“经贸汉语口语”系列教材

第4版
The Fourth Edition

BUSINESS CHINESE CONVERSATION (Elementary)

经贸初级汉语口语

上 I

主　编：黄为之
参加编写人员：杨廷治　陈　辉　黄锡之
杨天舒　成伟武

北京语言大学出版社
BEIJING LANGUAGE AND CULTURE UNIVERSITY PRESS

图书在版编目（CIP）数据

经贸初级汉语口语．上 / 黄为之主编 ；杨廷治等编写．— 4 版．— 北京 ：北京语言大学出版社，2017.12（2024.1 重印）

ISBN 978-7-5619-4971-9

Ⅰ.①经… Ⅱ.①黄… ②杨… Ⅲ.①贸易－汉语－口语－对外汉语教学－教材 Ⅳ.① H195.4

中国版本图书馆 CIP 数据核字 (2017) 第 247523 号

经贸初级汉语口语（第 4 版）· 上

JINGMAO CHUJI HANYU KOUYU (DI 4 BAN) · SHANG

排版制作：北京创艺涵文化发展有限公司
责任印制：周 燚

出版发行：北京语言大学出版社
社　　址：北京市海淀区学院路 15 号，100083
网　　址：www.blcup.com
电子信箱：service@blcup.com
电　　话：编辑部　8610-82303390
　　　　　国内发行　8610-82303650/3591/3648
　　　　　海外发行　8610-82303365/3080/3668
　　　　　北语书店　8610-82303653
　　　　　网购咨询　8610-82303908
印　　刷：北京虎彩文化传播有限公司

版　　次：2017 年 12 月第 4 版　　印　　次：2024 年 1 月第 5 次印刷
开　　本：787 毫米 × 1092 毫米　1/16　　印　　张：18.5　插表 1
字　　数：323 千字
定　　价：55.00 元

PRINTED IN CHINA

凡有印装质量问题，本社负责调换。售后QQ号1367565611，电话010-82303590

第四版前言

当前，中国经济已经高度融合于世界经济体系，中国倡导的合作共赢、打造全球命运共同体的理念，越来越具有世界影响，中国经济在更高层次上的新一轮改革开放格局，已经形成。“一带一路”的建设对亚欧非乃至全世界经济产生重大影响；“亚投行”作为开放包容、互联互通的成果，助力于亚洲经济圈发展；“中国制造”涌现出众多高端名牌产品，引起了全世界的关注和争购；中国企业走向世界，成为全球资本市场最活跃的投资生力军；“互联网+”的万众创新，日益改变着社会经济形态和生活方式。所有这一切，正在深刻改变世界经济和国际贸易格局。我们的经贸汉语教材，应该对这种新常态、新趋势、新情况，做出及时反映和解读，这对外国留学生了解中国的现实情况，会有很大帮助。

本次修订版保留了原书的体例和基本内容，增加了四篇新课文，修改了部分课文，增加了一些练习。

黄为之

2017年6月

Preface to the Fourth Edition

At present, China's economy has been highly integrated in the world economic system and embraces a new round of reform and opening up at a higher level, with its concept of win-win cooperation and global community of common destiny enjoying greater influence around the world. The Belt and Road initiative exerts deep influence on Asia, Europe, Africa and even the whole world. The Asian Infrastructure Investment Bank, as a result of openness, inclusiveness, and interconnection, promotes the development of the economic circle of Asia; with the emergence of many high-end brand-name products, "Made in China" attracts so much attention that people rush to buy them; Chinese enterprises reach out to the world and become the most active investment force in global capital market; the innovative "Internet +" changes social and economic patterns and lifestyles day by day. As a result, the world economy and international trade pattern undergo profound changes. Our business Chinese textbooks should reflect and interpret the new normal, new trend and new situation in a timely manner so as to help foreign students in understanding China's reality.

The revised edition, on the basis of the original style and basic content, modifies some texts and adds four new ones and some exercises.

Huang Weizhi

June, 2017

第三版前言

这次“经贸汉语口语”系列教材再版，主要作了四方面的修改：

一、《经贸初级汉语口语》上册，原来只有 1 ～ 10 课的课文配有拼音课文，现在根据外国留学生的要求，为了初学者学习口语的方便，增补了后 16 课的拼音课文；下册每课练习最后一题的小故事，对初学者也有一定的难度，这次修改也一并删去了。

二、世界发展很快，为能与时俱进，修改一些陈旧了的信息是必要的，如改“对外经济贸易合作部”为“商务部”，改“欧洲共同体”为“欧洲联盟”，改“关贸总协定”为“世贸组织”；欧元流通以后，法国法郎、德国马克等已不再流通，也作了相应修改；书中引用的各种数据，有许多变化，凡是能查到的，都修改征引了最新资料，等等。

三、修改了部分课文、注释和练习，以反映社会生活和经济生活的巨大变化。

四、修订了一些打字排版的错误和书写不规范之处。

这次修订一定还有不尽如人意的地方，欢迎专家、同行、外国朋友和留学生指正。

对外经济贸易大学

黄为之

2006 年 5 月

Preface to the Third Edition

The major changes of this edition of *Business Chinese Conversation* include the following four parts:

Firstly, as only texts in the first 10 lessons of *Business Chinese Conversation (Elementary)* were supplied with *pinyin* in the previous editions, *pinyin* texts of the other 16 lessons have been added for the convenience of foreign Chinese beginners. Short stories in the last exercise of each lesson in Book Two are deleted to decrease the difficulty for beginners.

Secondly, changing old terms is necessary along with the development of the world. For example, "Ministry of Foreign Trade and Economic Cooperation" has been changed into "Ministry of Commerce", "European Communities" into "European Union" and "General Agreement on Tariffs and Trade" into "World Trade Organization". As francs and marks are taken out of circulation, they are replaced by euros.

Thirdly, some of the texts, notes and exercises have been revised so as to mirror the great changes in social and economic lives.

Fourthly, some typos and nonstandard writings have been corrected.

We realize that this edition is not free of errors and shortcomings, and suggestions from experts, fellow teachers, foreign friends and students are welcome.

Huang Weizhi
University of International
Business and Economics,
May, 2006

再版前言

《经贸初级汉语口语》，1993年出版后，受到社会各界的热烈欢迎，被各院校和自学者广泛采用。出版的这些年来，中国的国际贸易形势发生了很大变化，有许多新的内容、新的语言需要学习；在教学实践中，我们也积累了经验，听取了各方面的意见，觉得对这本口语教材，现在进行修订、再版，是适时的。

1999年新版《经贸初级汉语口语》，在保持初版体例和优点的基础上，作了较大的修改。全书从原来的36课增加到50课，由一册分为上、下册，原有的内容作了调整，增加了经贸领域出现的新话题、新词语；减缓了学习进程的坡度，由浅入深、循序渐进的教学原则，得到了更充分的体现。我们相信，这个新版本，会在更高的水准上满足教师和学习者的需要。

1999年新版《经贸初级汉语口语》的英语翻译是黄震华教授。

对外经济贸易大学
黄为之
1999年2月

Preface to the Second Edition

Since its publication in 1993, *Business Chinese Conversation (Elementary)* has been well-received by various circles of the society, and adopted as a textbook by many universities and colleges and self-taught learners. The situation of China's international trade has witnessed great changes during the past years, which means that there are lots of new things to learn. In our teaching practice, we have also accumulated first-hand experiences and listened to suggestions from all sources. We feel that it is the right time now to revise and republish this book.

The 1999 edition of *Business Chinese Conversation (Elementary)*, while keeping the format and merits of the first edition, has undergone major and comprehensive revision. The number of lessons has been increased from 36 to 50, and the new edition consists of two volumes. The contents have also been adjusted, with new topics and new expressions in the arena of trade and economy added, and the difficulty lowered so that the progressive instruction is exemplified. We believe that the new edition will be better able to meet the needs of the teachers and learners.

The English translator of the 1999 edition of *Business Chinese Conversation (Elementary)* is Professor Huang Zhenhua.

Huang Weizhi
University of International
Business and Economics,
February, 1999

原版前言

初级教材的适用对象是从零开始的初学者。

留学生学习汉语有他们自身的特殊性。一方面，他们对汉语一无所知，没有听说汉语的能力；另一方面，他们又大多是成年人，有充分发达的智能、丰富的社会阅历和科学知识；他们没有孩子那样强的语言模仿力，而同时又具有孩子不可比拟的理解力和接受力。留学生的这个特殊性，在汉语学习过程中，形成一对突出的矛盾。它一方面要求教师注意学生的零起点特点，必须像教孩子学话一样，从一字一词教起，学生也必须从一字一词学起，学习必然存在着一个日积月累、循序渐进的过程；另一方面，它又要求教师充分注意到学生的成人特点，在教学过程中，不要把学生简单地当学话的孩子对待，而应该运用各种手段调动学生的主观能动性，发挥他们的智能、阅历和知识优势，使他们既学得扎实，又学得快捷。如何认识留学生学习汉语的这种特殊性，并把这种认识运用在教材编写和教学过程中，过去往往被人们忽略。教学内容和教学进度的超前或滞后，是常有的现象。我们在编写这本初级口语时，考虑到上述情况，试图解决好留学生在学习汉语中存在的这种矛盾性，使教与学都取得最理想的效果。

初级教材具有下面一些特点：

一至四课集中学习汉语拼音，这是为零起点的初学者编写的。来自东方国家的留学生，声母和韵母的发音难点较多；而来自西方国家的留学生，声调语调的问题则较突出。这四课中，有针对性地编入了大量练习。五至十课，还有拼音练习，以巩固前四课的学习成果。通过严格的教学实践，学生就可以比较好地解决这些语音问题，为学好标准的普通话打下坚实基础。

初级教材是经贸专业汉语教材。教材内容与常见的普通汉语教材内容有极大不同。普通汉语教材中，日常衣食住行和校园生活内容，占有相当大比重，本教材则把其中的有用部分与日常经济生活巧妙地结合了起来，而以经济生活为主要内容。日常经济生活，包括买卖东西、讨价还价、货物挑选、商业服务、销售广告、经营特色、公关工作、推销技巧等，内容丰富，涉及面广，切近生活，实际有用，而教材的词汇、句型及难易程度，又都与初学者的实际水平相当。

初级教材根据语言有交际情景与交际功能属性的原理，采用了课内与课外相结合的教学体系。从第五课开始，每两课一个专题。换句话说，我们把日常经济生活分为若干个层面，每一个层面，都用两篇课文来认识它、表述它。课文“在课内”，是在教师指导下的学习。这是闭门操练，务求根基扎实。课文“在课外”，是学生走出课堂，参与社会实践。这是亲自下海，在游泳中学游泳，意在复习和运用课堂学到的语言知识。两篇课文，内容紧密相关而天地各不相同。学生学完并掌握了这两篇课文，也就学到了经济生活中一个层面的日常用语。这种教学体系，冲出了封闭式的课堂。教师在组织每一个专题课时，都可以要求学生在课前或课后，去参加相应的社会实践，为这一个专题的教学做课前准备或课后复习。本教材在进入教学过程后，必将以它生动活泼的教学形式，引起学生的极大兴趣，充分调动起学习积极性，发挥出成年人的学习优势，取得预期的效果。

初级教材在教学安排上，采用了低起点、大容量、高密度、分阶段而又大步推进的强化训练教学法。每一篇课文，生词量和篇幅长度，都超出了常见的同级普通汉语课本；整个教学过程，都以学生为主，课内课外的一切活动，都要求学生主动积极地去完成，教师只是参与、启发、引导，而决不作教授式的讲演。教学活动的单调、缓慢，学生学习的被动、疲沓，都是影响教学质量的不利因素。本教材提供了强化训练的丰富素材和各种手段，教师可以充分利用这些素材和手段，激发学生的强烈学习欲望和潜在能力，使学生进入学习的兴奋状态和紧张状态。我们所说的“紧张状态”，绝不排斥生动活泼、趣味盎然的教学气氛。恰恰相反，这种教学气氛越浓，学生也就越兴奋、越投入，知识的学习与运用也就越能达到最佳境界，一切看似不可能一下学会的东西，就有可能在最短的时间里学到手，甚至运用得熟巧。

这本教材，从内容到形式，都走了一条新路子，肯定是不完善、不成熟的，还需要在今后的教学实践中作更深入的探索，希望能听到同行教师和留学生们的批评意见。

初级教材参加编写的人员还有杨廷治、陈辉、黄锡之、杨天舒、杨立群、苏伯华、成伟武等同志，我校副校长黄震华教授负责全书的英文注释和翻译。加拿大籍专家 David Packer 先生校阅了课文译文。我校校长孙维炎教授最后审定了全书。国家对外汉语教学领导小组办公室的领导同志，对本教材的编写与出版给予了指导和帮助。我校校领导、出版社和外事处的同志们，都给本教材的出版以大力支持。在此，我对他们表示由衷的感谢。

对外经济贸易大学

黄为之

1993 年 1 月

Preface to the First Edition

This textbook is meant for Chinese beginners.

Foreign students learning the Chinese language have their own specific characteristics. On the one hand, they know nothing about Chinese, and they do not have the listening comprehension and speaking abilities concerning this target language. On the other hand, most of them are adults with fully-developed intellects, rich social experience and scientific knowledge. They do not have a language imitation ability as strong as children, but at the same time, they have an understanding and receptive abilities with which children cannot compare. These characteristics are, in a way, contradictory. Teachers are required to pay attention to the fact that their students are starting from scratch, and they have to begin their teaching from simple words, just like teaching children to speak. Students have to start their learning from simple words too. Learning is also a process of accumulation. The characteristics of the learners also require the teachers to pay attention to the fact that their students are adults, and they cannot be treated as children. The teachers have to use every means to bring the students' initiative into full play, mobilizing their advantages in intelligence, experience and knowledge, so that they can learn solid knowledge quickly. The question of how to understand the special characteristics of foreign students learning Chinese and to utilize such knowledge in the compilation of textbooks and in the teaching process has often been neglected. It has frequently been the case that the content and teaching schedule have been either too advanced or lagging behind. In writing this book of elementary Chinese conversation, we have taken these aspects into consideration, trying to resolve the aforementioned contradictions in the foreign students' Chinese learning process, so as to bring about the most satisfactory results in both learning and teaching.

The present textbook has the following characteristics:

Lessons one to four concentrate on the learning of the Chinese phonetic alphabet or *pinyin*. This is for the benefit of beginners. Students coming from Oriental countries have more difficulties in the pronunciation of vowels and consonants, while those from Western countries have their main problems in tones and intonation. These four lessons contain a large number of exercises aiming at such problems. Phonological exercises continue in lessons five to ten, with a view to consolidating what was learned in the first four lessons. Through strict learning and teaching practice, students can solve these phonological problems, laying a solid foundation for mastering *Putonghua* (standard Chinese).

This textbook is a Chinese teaching material for business purpose, the content of which is very different from those of ordinary textbooks, where a large proportion is devoted to such daily matters as food, clothing, shelter, means of travel, and the life on campus. The present book endeavors to combine the useful parts of the above mentioned topics with those daily business routines such as buying and selling, bargaining, selection of goods, commercial services, advertising, special features of management, public relations, salesmanship, etc. Emphasis is placed on these aspects and the content is such that the students are exposed to a broad range of knowledge that is realistic and practical. The book's vocabulary, sentence structures, and the difficulty are suitable for beginners.

According to the principle that language has such properties as communicative situation and communicative functions, this book has adopted a system of combining learning in class and after class. Starting from Lesson Five, there are two lessons for each topic. More specifically, daily business life is divided into several parts, each of which is presented in two lessons. The "in-class" text is for learning under the teacher's instruction. It is closed-door practice, aimed at laying a solid foundation. The "after-class" text is for students to learn when they participate in social practice. As the saying goes, this is "going into the sea and learning how to swim by swimming". Its purpose is to review and use the linguistic knowledge that has been learned in class. The contents of the two texts are closely related, but with different fields of activities. When the students have learned and mastered both texts, they have also learned the daily expressions for one aspect of "economic life". This teaching system has broken down the closed-end teaching approach. In organizing the teaching of a topic, the teacher can always ask the students to take part in the corresponding social practice either before or after class, as a preview or review of the topic. After entering into the teaching process, the content of this textbook, with its active and lively teaching style, will arouse great interest among the students, motivate them to learn, and take into account the extraordinary learning capabilities of adults, so as to achieve the expected results.

The present textbook adopts the teaching method for intensive training characterized by low threshold, large volume of content, high density, and staged and quick progressing in teaching. The number of new words and the length of the texts have both exceeded those of the ordinary Chinese textbooks. The whole teaching process is student-centred. Students are required to accomplish both the in-class and the after-class activities before they proceed. The teacher's role is to participate, inspire, and guide, but never lecture. The monotony and slow pace in the teaching and learning activities, and the passiveness and slackness on the part of the students are negative factors affecting the learning result. This textbook provides ample materials and means for intensified training, which can be fully utilized by the teachers to stimulate the students' strong desire and potential to learn. Students respond to a lively and interesting learning atmosphere. The better the learning atmosphere, the more excited and absorbed the students will become. Hence the optimal state will be attained for learning and use of knowledge. Things that seem impossible to learn will be mastered within the shortest period of time by the students.

As this textbook follows a new path in both its content and form, errors and shortcomings are inevitable. Further exploration is needed in future teaching practice. Therefore, criticisms and suggestions from fellow teachers and foreign students are highly welcome.

Those who participated in the compilation of the textbook include Yang Tingzhi, Chen Hui, Huang Xizhi, Yang Tianshu, Yang Liqun, Su Bohua, Cheng Weiwu. The English translation of all the texts and explanations has been done by Professor Huang Zhenhua, vice president of University of International Business and Economics (UIBE). Mr. David Packer, a Canadian expert working at UIBE, assisted with the English translation. And finally Professor Sun Weiyan, president of UIBE, examined the manuscript of the whole book. Senior members from the National Office for Teaching Chinese as a Foreign Language have provided guidance and support for the compilation and publication of the book. Leading members of UIBE, and colleagues from UIBE Press and Foreign Affairs Office have also given substantial support to this book. I hereby extend my heartfelt thanks to all of them.

Huang Weizhi
University of International
Business and Economics,
January, 1993

使用说明

对外汉语教学有许多特点。就学习者来说，他们来自不同国家，不同民族，有不同经历和不同文化背景，在学习汉语时，会明显表现出各自的特殊性和彼此的差异性；就教师来说，每一个教师，都有自己的教学个性和教学经历，教学风格和教学方法。鉴于此，不可能有一个整齐划一的教法与学法，我们这里的“使用说明”，仅仅是一个建议，供使用这套“经贸汉语口语”的教师和学习者参考。事实上，许多问题已经在这套书各册的前言中说到了，这里就不再重复，现在只作如下几点补充说明。

这套“经贸汉语口语”虽然是从零学起，但它“采用了低起点、大容量、高密度、分阶段而又大步推进的强化训练教学法”。从上面一段话，我们知道，这套书涉及的内容很广，又有相当的难度，一个学期大致要学完一册书，因此，预习和复习，就显得特别重要，尤其是预习，学生更要多花些时间，多下些功夫。像课文中的生词和语法点，书中已有简明扼要的注释，学生可以自学习得，教师只需讲解其中的难点，做些熟巧练习；每一篇课文，应要求学生在预习时，通过学习生词和参看课文的英语翻译，能比较顺畅地阅读下来并基本理解，教师可通过师生互相问答，检验学生阅读与理解的程度，讲解其中的疑难问题；课文中有关文化知识的注释及课文后的一篇短文，也要以自学为主。有些练习，也当做如是处理。不要把有限的课堂时间耗费在课文及相关材料的阅读上，要以课文和这些材料为“谈资”，开展生动活泼的谈话；“大容量”，要求许多东西在课下消化；“高密度”，则要求合理有效地利用时间，强化口语训练。总之，教师与学习者，都要有一个牢固意识，这是一部口语教材，练习口语，习得一口流利的汉语，是这套教材的终极目的。

与上述问题相关的，是在教与学的过程中，如何抓住重点。以这套书的《经贸中级汉语口语》和《经贸高级汉语口语》为例，每一课都是生词量大，内容多，篇幅也相对长，试图在一个教学单元时间里（4～6课时），把课文中出现的全部生词和全部内容都学会、都掌握，一般来说，几乎是不可能的。要善于根据课文题目的提示，找出每一课的关键词、重点句和核心内容，学会和掌握这些关键词、重点句和核心内容即可，其余的，在以后的重现中会逐渐习得和熟悉。教材在编写过程中，十分重视新知识的重现率和温故而知新的学习渐进性，老师和学习者都不需担心顾此失彼。

《经贸初级汉语口语》上、下册一共54课，每课4课时，一周6课时；《经贸中级汉语口语》上、下册一共40课，每课4～6课时，一周6课时；《经贸高级汉语口语》上、下册一共32课，每课4课时，一周4课时。如果条件允许，尽可能多安排一些课外实践活动。如《经贸初级汉语口语》，每一个话题都有“课上”和“课外”两篇课文，在学习“课外”一篇课文前，一定要学生走出去，学生在社会上会得到许多新鲜的东西，“课外”课文就变活了；学习《经贸中级汉语口语》时，可以组织去观摩正式谈判，或观看正式谈判录像，也可以到市场演练货物贸易谈判，有做生意经历的学生还可以现身说法；学习《经贸高级汉语口语》时，可围绕一个文化专题组织一些参观、访问和座谈活动。社会实践方式是多种多样的，这里只是举例而已，目的是要把死的文字材料变成活的知识，变成学生可以自由表达的口语能力。

对外经济贸易大学
黄为之
2016年5月

Users' Guide

Teaching Chinese as a foreign language has its own characteristics. The learners are from different countries of different ethnic groups with different life experience and cultural background and display their own characteristics in learning Chinese, while the teachers too have their own teaching characteristics, experiences, styles and methods. Considering this diversity, we do not want to offer a standardized teaching and learning method to use this series of Chinese textbooks. However, we'd like to offer some suggestions for teachers and learners. Since some questions have been discussed in the Preface, we only address several additional points here.

Business Chinese Conversation adopts the teaching method for intensive training characterized by low threshold, large volume of content, high density, and staged and quick progressing in teaching. With a wide range of topics, the content of certain difficulty and the curriculum requirement to finish one volume within a term, it attaches particular importance to the preview and review. Especially for preview, students should spend more time and efforts on new words and grammar points and try to learn on their own with the aid of explanations and English translation of the texts. They should read through the texts and gain basic understanding before class. Then in class the teacher can use "questions and answers" to examine their reading comprehension, and will only need to explain the difficult points. The notes on cultural knowledge and the short essays at the end of the lesson should also be learned by students themselves. Some of the exercises should also be handled this way. Don't waste class hours on reading the texts and related materials, which should instead be the "lead" to lively dialogues among the students. "Large volume of content" indicates that lots of content have to be digested after class; "high density" requires effective use of time and intensive training of speaking. All in all, teachers and learners together should be aware that this is a series of textbooks for practicing speaking with the ultimate goal to enable learners to speak fluent Chinese.

Closely related to these questions is the question of how to grasp the key points during teaching and learning. Take *Business Chinese Conversation* (*Intermediate*) and *Business Chinese Conversation* (*Advanced*) of this series for example. In each lesson there are a large number of new words, rich content, and texts of longer length. The attempt to master all the new words and content within a teaching unit (4-6 class hours) is almost impossible. Therefore, students should be able to focus on key words, important sentences and core content of each lesson according to the hint of its title. As for the rest, they will achieve the mastery of them in their later reappearance. During the compilation, we put a lot of emphasis on the reoccurring rate of new knowledge and the progressiveness of learning, so the teachers and learners can rest assured of our arrangement.

Altogether the two volumes of *Business Chinese Conversation (Elementary)* have 54 lessons, with four class hours for each lesson and six class hours each week. The two volumes of *Business Chinese Conversation (Intermediate)* have 40 lessons, with four to six class hours for each lesson and six class hours each week. And the two volumes of *Business Chinese Conversation (Advanced)* have 32 lessons, with four class hours for each lesson and four class hours each week. If possible, please arrange extracurricular activities as many as possible. For example, in *Business Chinese Conversation (Elementary)*, there are usually one text for "in-class learning" and the other for "after-class learning" under each topic. Before learning the latter one, ask the students to go outside, and they can bring in lots of fresh stuff which will enliven the learning. While teaching *Business Chinese Conversation (Intermediate)*, the teacher can arrange students to watch a real negotiation or one on the video; students can go to practice trade negotiation themselves; and those with experience in doing business can also talk about their own stories about negotiation. While teaching *Business Chinese Conversation (Advanced)*, a variety of social activities like visits, discussion, etc. are also encouraged. Our purpose is to turn the "dead" language materials into "live" knowledge, and further into the students' ability to express themselves freely in Chinese.

Huang Weizhi
University of International
Business and Economics,
May, 2016

目录

Contents

第一课 Lesson 1 你好 Hello 1

第二课 Lesson 2 他是谁 Who Is He 11

第三课 Lesson 3 我的朋友 My Friends 21

第四课 Lesson 4 怎么称呼 How to Address a Person 30

第五课 Lesson 5 打电话 Making Telephone Calls 38

第六课 Lesson 6 预订房间 Booking a Room 46

第七课 Lesson 7 换钱 Changing Money 53

第八课 Lesson 8 出租车 Taxi 60

第九课 Lesson 9 他没来上班 He Has Not Turned up for Work 67

第十课 Lesson 10 今天是她的生日 It Is Her Birthday Today 74

第十一课 Lesson 11 你想做什么（一） What Do You Want to Do（Ⅰ） 83

第十二课 Lesson 12 你想做什么（二） What Do You Want to Do（Ⅱ） 91

第十三课 Lesson 13 你会说中国话吗（一） Can You Speak Chinese（Ⅰ） 99

第十四课 Lesson 14 你会说中国话吗（二） Can You Speak Chinese（Ⅱ） 107

第十五课 Lesson 15 你会买东西吗（一） Do You Know How to Make Purchases（Ⅰ） 115

第十六课 Lesson 16 你会买东西吗（二） Do You Know How to Make Purchases（Ⅱ） 121

第十七课 Lesson 17 我们离不开它（一） We Can't Do Without It（Ⅰ） 129

第十八课 Lesson 18 我们离不开它（二） We Can't Do Without It（II） 136

第十九课 Lesson 19 她怎么了（一） What's the Matter with Her（I） 144

第二十课 Lesson 20 她怎么了（二） What's the Matter with Her（II） 152

第二十一课 Lesson 21 是谁的错（一） Whose Fault Is It（I） 161

第二十二课 Lesson 22 是谁的错（二） Whose Fault Is It（II） 170

第二十三课 Lesson 23 住在哪儿（一） Where Do You Live（I） 178

第二十四课 Lesson 24 住在哪儿（二） Where Do You Live（II） 186

第二十五课 Lesson 25 今天怎么样（一） What's the Weather Like Today（I） 195

第二十六课 Lesson 26 今天怎么样（二） What's the Weather Like Today（II） 203

第二十七课 Lesson 27 逛北京（一） Going Sightseeing in Beijing（I） 212

第二十八课 逛北京（二） 222
Lesson 28 Going Sightseeing in Beijing（II）

英译课文 231
English Translation of the Texts

生词总表 257
Vocabulary List

1

第一课 你好
Lesson 1 Hello

学拼音
The Phonetic Alphabet (Ⅰ)

一、声母（一）Initial consonants (Ⅰ)

b p m f d t n l

二、韵母（一）Vowels (Ⅰ)

ɑ o e er i u ü

1. 拼读练习 Combine sounds into syllables.

	ɑ	o	e	i	u	ü
b	bɑ	bo		bi	bu	
p	pɑ	po		pi	pu	
m	mɑ	mo	me	mi	mu	
f	fɑ	fo			fu	
d	dɑ		de	di	du	
t	tɑ		te	ti	tu	
n	nɑ		ne	ni	nu	nü
l	lɑ		le	li	lu	lü

2. 辨音练习 Distinguish the sounds.

ba——pa　bo——po　bi——pi　bu——pu　da——ta
de——te　di——ti　du——tu　na——la　ne——le
ni——li　nu——lu　nü——lü

三、声母（二）Initial consonants（II）

j　q　x　g　k　h

1. 拼读练习 Combine sounds into syllables.

	a	o	e	i	u	ü
j				ji		ju
q				qi		qu
x				xi		xu
g	ga		ge		gu	
k	ka		ke		ku	
h	ha		he		hu	

2. 辨音练习 Distinguish the sounds.

ji——ju　ji——qi　ji——xi　ju——qu　ju——xu
qu——xu　qi——xu　qi——xi　qi——qu　xi——ju
xi——qu　xi——xu

ga——ka　ge——ke　gu——ku　ka——ha　ke——he
ku——hu　ha——ga　he——ge　hu——gu　ga——ge
ke——ku　he——hu

四、韵母（二）Vowels（II）

ai ei ao ou an en ang eng ong

1. 拼读练习 Combine sounds into syllables.

	ai	ei	ao	ou	an	en	ang	eng	ong
b	bai	bei	bao		ban	ben	bang	beng	
p	pai	bei	pao	pou	pan	pen	pang	peng	
m	mai	mei	mao	mou	man	men	mang	meng	
f		fei		fou	fan	fen	fang	feng	
d	dai	dei	dao	dou	dan	den	dang	deng	dong
t	tai	tei	tao	tou	tan		tang	teng	tong
n	nai	nei	nao	nou	nan	nen	nang	neng	nong
l	lai	lei	lao	lou	lan		lang	leng	long
g	gai	gei	gao	gou	gan	gen	gang	geng	gong
k	kai	kei	kao	kou	kan	ken	kang	keng	kong
h	hai	hei	hao	hou	han	hen	hang	heng	hong

2. 辨音练习 Distinguish the sounds.

bai——pai　bei——pei　bao——pao　ban——pan
dai——tai　dao——tao　dou——tou　dan——tan
nai——lai　nao——lao　nou——lou　nan——lan
gai——kai　gao——kao　gou——hou　gan——kan
bang——pang　beng——peng　dang——tang　deng——teng
dong——tong　gang——kang　geng——keng　gong——kong

五、声调 Tones

声调练习 Practice the tones.

ā á ǎ à　　ō ó ǒ ò　　ē é ě è

ī í ǐ ì　　ū ú ǔ ù　　ǖ ǘ ǚ ǜ

mā	má	mǎ	mà	bā	bá	bǎ	bà	dī	dí	dǐ	dì
gē	gé	gě	gè	nī	ní	nǐ	nì	wō	wó	wǒ	wò
yē	yé	yě	yè	hēn	hén	hěn	hèn	hāo	háo	hǎo	hào

课文 Text

1. A：你好！
   Nǐ hǎo!
   B：你好！
   Nǐ hǎo!

2. A：小姐，你好！
   Xiǎojiě, nǐ hǎo!
   B：你好！
   Nǐ hǎo!

3. A：嗨，安娜，你好！
   Hēi, Ānnà, nǐ hǎo!
   B：你好，杰克！
   Nǐ hǎo, Jiékè!

4. A: 安娜， 早上 好！
Ānnà， zǎoshang hǎo!

B: 早上 好，杰克！
Zǎoshang hǎo， Jiékè!

5. A: 嗨，安娜！
Hēi， Ānnà!

B: 嗨，杰克！
Hēi， Jiékè!

A: 你 好 吗？
Nǐ hǎo ma?

B: 谢谢，我 很 好！你 呢？
Xièxie， wǒ hěn hǎo! Nǐ ne?

A: 我 也 很 好！
Wǒ yě hěn hǎo!

生 词 New Words

1. 你	nǐ	you
2. 好	hǎo	good, fine, well
3. 小姐	xiǎojiě	Miss
4. 嗨	hēi	hi, hey
5. 早上	zǎoshang	morning
6. 吗	ma	*an auxiliary word used at the end of a question*
7. 谢谢	xièxie	to thank you; thanks
8. 我	wǒ	I, me
9. 很	hěn	very

10. 呢	ne	*a particle often used at the end of a special, alternative, or rhetorical question to indicate a question*
11. 也	yě	too, also, as well, either

专 名 Proper Nouns

1. 安娜	Ānnà	Anna
2. 杰克	Jiékè	Jack

注 释 Notes

1 现代汉语可以用拼音记音。现代汉语拼音共有 21 个声母，38 个韵母。汉语的音节大多是由声母和韵母拼合成的。有的音节，只有韵母，没有声母。

Modern Chinese uses the phonetic alphabet or *pinyin* to record the pronunciation. There are altogether 21 initial consonants and 38 vowels. Most Chinese syllables are formed by initial consonants and simple or compound vowels. Some syllables have only vowels and no initial consonants.

2 声调：汉语的每一个音节都有声调，声调有区别语义的作用，相同的音节，声调不同，语义也不同。现代汉语普通话有四个基本声调，声调名称和符号是 ˉ（第一声），ˊ（第二声），ˇ（第三声），ˋ（第四声）。各声调调值分别为：ˉ（55），ˊ（35），ˇ（214），ˋ（51），图示如下：

Tones: Every Chinese syllable has a tone, which has the function of distinguishing semantic meanings. The same syllable with different tones differs in semantic meaning. *Putonghua* (standard Chinese) of modern Chinese has four basic tones. The names and marks for these tones are: ˉ (the first tone), ˊ (the second tone), ˇ (the third one), ˋ (the fourth tone). The pitches of the four tones are as follows: ˉ (55), ˊ (35), ˇ (214), and ˋ (51). It is indicated in the diagram:

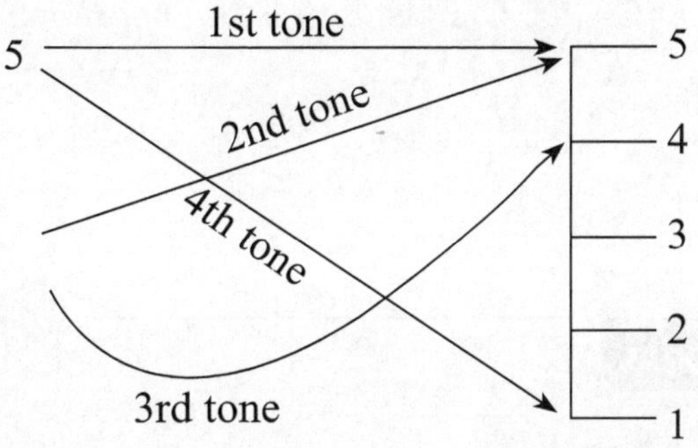

3 “吗、呢”都是语气助词。用“吗”表示疑问语气，可用在是非问句的末尾。例如：

吗 and 呢 are both modal particles. 吗 is used to mark the interrogative mood. It is placed at the end of a yes-no question. For example:

A：你好吗？

B：我很好。（我不好。）

用“呢”也可表示疑问语气，可用来承接上面的话提出问题。例如：

呢 also indicates the interrogative mood. It continues with the previous topic and raises a question. For example:

A：你好吗？

B：我很好。你呢？

A：我也很好。

4 本课课文有五组对话，是常用的五种问候方式。第一种，认识的人或不认识的人见面，都可以这样互致问候。第二种，用于问候不认识的人，称呼对方“小姐”“先生”，是对对方的尊敬，比较礼貌、客气。第三种，用于认识的朋友、同学、同事，所以可以称呼对方的名字。第四种，是受西方国家影响流行起来的一种问候方式。第五种，是用疑问句形式表达问候。

The text of this lesson consists of five dialogues, which are the five most common ways of greeting. The first is used either between strangers or between people who are acquainted with each other. The second is used to greet a stranger. To use 小姐 or 先生 is a polite way to address the other party and show one's respect. The third is used between friends, fellow students, or colleagues. So you can call the other party by their names. The fourth is a greeting in the West, but it has become quite popular in China. The last one is to use an interrogative sentence for greeting.

补充生词
Additional New Words

1. 爸爸	bàba	father
2. 妈妈	māma	mother
3. 哥哥	gēge	elder brother
4. 弟弟	dìdi	younger brother
5. 姐姐	jiějie	elder sister
6. 妹妹	mèimei	younger sister
7. 先生	xiānsheng	mister, gentleman, sir, husband
8. 老师	lǎoshī	teacher
9. 下午	xiàwǔ	afternoon
10. 晚上	wǎnshang	evening, night

练　习
Exercises

一、替换练习。
Substitution drills.

A：小姐，你好！
B：你好！

先生　　老师

A：你好，杰克！
B：你好！

安娜　姐姐　哥哥　妹妹

A：安娜，早上好！　　爸爸　妈妈　先生　老师
B：早上好。

A：杰克，你好吗？　　哥哥　姐姐　弟弟　爸爸　安娜
B：谢谢，我很好！你呢？
A：我也很好。

二、用拼音写出不同问候方式并熟读。

Write out different greetings in *pinyin* and read them repeatedly.

三、为下列单词写拼音并组句熟读。

Write the *pinyin* of the following words, make sentences with them, and read them repeatedly.

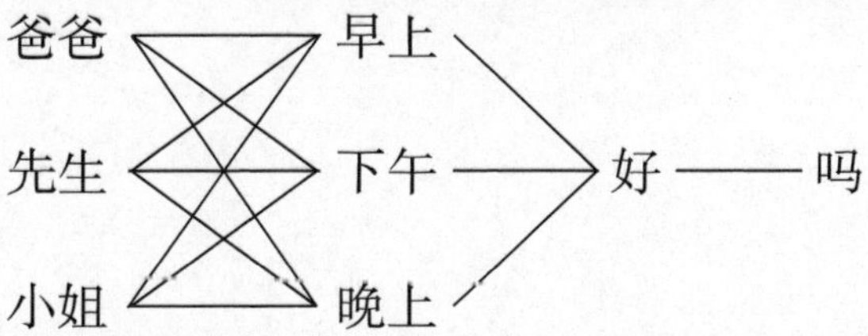

四、为下图写拼音，组句。

Write the *pinyin* of the following words, and make sentences with them.

老师
先生
小姐
爸爸
妈妈
姐姐
哥哥
弟弟
妹妹

也	很	好
3	2	1

2+1
老师很好。
3+1
老师也好。
3+2+1
老师也很好。

五、把下面的词组成句子。

Rearrange the following words into sentences.

1. 你　小姐　好
2. 先生　好　早上
3. 很　好　我　也
4. 你　很　也　吗　好

六、写课内生词并注拼音。

Copy the new words of the text and give the *pinyin* of each word.

2

第二课　他是谁
Lesson 2　Who Is He

学 拼 音
The Phonetic Alphabet (II)

一、声母 (一) Initial consonants (I)

z　c　s　zh　ch　sh　r

1. 拼读练习 Combine sounds into syllables.

	a	o	e	-i[ɿ]	-i[ʅ]	ai	ei	ong
z	za		ze	zi		zai	zei	zong
o	ca		ce	ci		cai		cong
s	sa		se	si		sai		song
zh	zha		zhe		zhi	zhai	zhei	zhong
ch	cha		che		chi	chai		chong
sh	sha		she		shi	shai	shei	
r			re		ri			rong

2. 辨音练习 Distinguish the sounds.

za——ca　　za——sa　　ca——sa

ze——ce　　ze——se　　ce——se

zi——ci	zi——si	ci——si	cu——su
ri——ni	zi——ji	si——xi	ru——nu
za——zha	ze——zhe	zi——zhi	zu——zhu
ca——cha	ce——che	ci——chi	cu——chu
sa——sha	se——she	si——shi	su——shu
zao——zhao	zou——zhou	zan——zhan	zeng——zheng
cai——chai	cao——chao	cou——chou	cang——chang
sao——shao	sou——shou	san——shan	seng——sheng

二、韵母 Vowels

ia ie iao iou（iu）
ian in iang ing iong

1. 拼读练习 Combine sounds into syllables.

	ia	ie	iao	iou（iu）	ian	in	iang	ing	iong
b		bie	biao		bian	bin		bing	
p		pie	piao		pian	pin		ping	
m		mie	miao	miu	mian	min		ming	
d	dia	die	diao	diu	dian			ding	
t		tie	tiao		tian			ting	
n		nie	niao	niu	nian	nin	niang	ning	
l	lia	lie	liao	liu	lian	lin	liang	ling	
j	jia	jie	jiao	jiu	jian	jin	jiang	jing	jiong
q	qia	qie	qiao	qiu	qian	qin	qiang	qing	qiong
x	xia	xie	xiao	xiu	xian	xin	xiang	xing	xiong

2. 辨音练习 Distinguish the sounds.

bie——pie	biao——piao	bian——pian
die——tie	diao——tiao	dian——tian
jia——qia	jie——pie	jiu——qiu
bin——bing	pin——ping	min——ming
ding——ting	jing——qing	jiong——qiong
jiao——qiao	jian——qian	jiong——xiong

三、声调 Tones

声调练习 Practice the tones.

qīng qíng qǐng qìng / wēn wén wěn wèn } qǐngwèn (May I ask...)

zāi zái zǎi zài / jiān jián jiǎn jiàn } zàijiàn (goodbye)

zhōng zhóng zhǒng zhòng / guō guó guǒ guò } Zhōngguó (China)

bēi béi běi bèi / jīng jíng jǐng jìng } Běijīng (Beijing)

xiē xié xiě xiè——xièxie (to thank you)

gùkè (customer) miànbāo (bread)

niúnǎi (milk) qìchē (car)

tóngzhì (comrade) qīnmì (intimate)

hòutiān (the day after tomorrow) Xuěbì (Sprite)

zìdiǎn (dictionary) yǐzi (chair)

课 文

Text

1. A: 你 好！我 是 谢 文。
   Nǐ hǎo! Wǒ shì Xiè Wén.

   B: 你 好！我 是 安娜。
   Nǐ hǎo! Wǒ shì Ānnà.

   A: 很 高兴 认识 你！
   Hěn gāoxìng rènshi nǐ!

   B: 认识 你，我 也 很 高兴！
   Rènshi nǐ, wǒ yě hěn gāoxìng!

2. A: 你 是 经理 吗？
   Nǐ shì jīnglǐ ma?

   B: 不，我 是 秘书，他 是 经理。
   Bù, Wǒ shì mìshū, tā shì jīnglǐ.

   A: 啊，对不起！
   À, duìbuqǐ!

   B: 没 关系。
   Méi guānXi.

3. A: 经理，你 好！我 是 安娜。
   Jīnglǐ, nǐ hǎo! Wǒ shì Ānnà.

   B: 安娜 小姐，你 好！这 是 谁？
   Ānnà Xiǎojiě, nǐ hǎo! Zhè shì shéi?

   A: 这 是 朱丽亚。
   Zhè shì Zhūlìyà.

   C: 朱丽亚·利维，美国人。
   Zhūlìyà LìWéi, Měiguórén.

B: 你 好！很 高兴 认识 你！
Nǐ hǎo! Hěn gāoxìng rènshi nǐ!

C: 认识 你，我 也 很 高兴！
Rènshi nǐ, wǒ yě hěn gāoxìng!

4. A: 经理，早上 好！
Jīnglǐ, zǎoshang hǎo!

B: 早上 好，安娜！
Zǎoshang hǎo, Ānnà!

A: 我 是 朱丽亚。
Wǒ shì Zhūlìyà.

B: 啊，对。你 好，朱丽亚 夫人！
À, duì. Nǐ hǎo, Zhūlìyà fūren!

A: 小姐，朱丽亚·利维 小姐。
Xiǎojiě, Zhūlìyà Lìwéi xiǎojiě.

B: 啊，对不起，利维 小姐。
À, duìbuqǐ, Lìwéi xiǎojiě.

A: 没 关系。
Méi guānxi.

生 词
New Words

1. 他	tā	he, him
2. 是	shì	to be
3. 谁	shéi/shuí	who
4. 高兴	gāoxìng	glad, happy, pleased, cheerful
5. 认识	rènshi	to know
6. 经理	jīnglǐ	manager
7. 不	bù	no, not
8. 秘书	mìshū	secretary

9. 啊	à	eh, oh, ah
10. 对不起	duìbuqǐ	I'm sorry; to excuse me, to pardon me
11. 没关系	méi guānxi	it doesn't matter, that's all right, never mind
12. 这	zhè	this
13. 人	rén	man, person, people, human being
14. 对	duì	right, correct
15. 夫人	fūrén	wife, lady, Mrs., Madame

专　名　Proper Nouns

1. 谢文	Xiè Wén	Xie Wen
2. 朱丽亚·利维	Zhūlìyà Lìwéi	Julia Levy
3. 美国	Měiguó	the United States

注　释
Notes

1　注意单元音i和-i[ɿ]，-i[ʅ]的区别。单元音i是不圆唇舌面前元音。-i[ɿ]是不圆唇舌尖前元音，-i[ʅ]是不圆唇舌尖后元音。同z、c、s相拼合的是-i[ɿ]，同zh、ch、sh、r相拼合的是-i[ʅ]，二者不能互换。单元音i永远不出现在z、c、s、zh、ch、sh、r之后。

Please note the distinction between the single vowels i and -i[ɿ]/[ʅ]. i is a front unrounded palatal vowel. -i[ɿ] is a front unrounded apical vowel, and -i[ʅ] is a back unrounded apical vowel. The vowel which goes with z, c, s is -i[ɿ]. The one which goes with zh, ch, sh and r is -i[ʅ]. They are not interchangable. The monophthong i never appears after z, c, s, zh, ch, sh or r.

2　现代汉语的声调，除四个基本声调外，还有一个轻声。轻声字不标调号，读时声音又轻又短。例如：

In modern Chinese, apart from the four basic tones, there is a neutral tone, which does not bear any tone mark and whose pronunciation should be both light and short. For example:

爸爸	bàba
妈妈	māma
姐姐	jiějie
先生	xiānsheng
对不起	duìbuqǐ
没关系	méi guānxi

3 现代汉语普通话每一个音节的声调符号在书写时，都标在元音上方，当一个音节的韵母有两个或三个元音时，则标在开口度最大的元音上。如：hǎo、kǒu。

The tone mark for each syllable in *Putonghua* of modern Chinese is written on top of the vowel. When a syllable has two or three vowels, it is placed on top of the vowel that is most open, e.g., hǎo, kǒu.

4 “是”，动词，在句中做谓语，表示一种肯定的判断。下面是汉语中最常见的一种句子格式：主语 + 谓语 “是” + 宾语。例如：

是 is a verb which, when functioning as the predicate in a sentence, expresses a positive judgment. The following is one of the most frequently used sentence patterns in Chinese: “subject +是 (the predicate verb) +object”. For example:

1. 我是安娜。
2. 他是经理。
3. 她是美国人。
4. 杰克也是美国人。

“是”的否定形式是在“是”的前面加否定副词“不”。例如：

The negative form of 是 is to put the negative adverb 不 before 是. For example:

1. 她不是安娜。
2. 谢文不是经理。
3. 他不是老师。
4. 利维不是法国人。

补充生词
Additional New Words

1. 学生	xuéshēng	student
2. 她	tā	she, her
3. 哪	nǎ	which
4. 国	guó	country, state, nation
5. 中国	Zhōngguó	China
6. 英国	Yīngguó	the United Kingdom
7. 法国	Fǎguó	France
8. 俄罗斯	Éluósī	Russia
9. 日本	Rìběn	Japan
10. 韩国	Hánguó	Republic of Korea

练习
Exercises

一、替换练习。
Substitution drills.

A：他是谁？
B：他是杰克。
A：你好！杰克！很高兴认识你。
B：你好！我也很高兴认识你。

谢文	安娜	朱丽亚
经理	老师	

A：你是老师吗？
B：不，我是经理，他是老师。
A：对不起。
B：没关系。

杰克	谢文
哥哥	弟弟
秘书	经理

A：你是美国人吗？
B：不，我不是美国人，我是英国人。
A：认识你很高兴。
B：我也很高兴。

法国	俄罗斯
日本	韩国
日本	中国

二、完成对话。

Complete the following dialogues.

A：你是谁？
B：________________。
A：你是美国人吗？
B：________________。

A：你夫人是中国人吗？
B：________________。
A：对不起。
B：________________。

A：小姐是哪国人？
B：________________。
A：认识你很高兴。
B：________________。

三、用下列词语填空、组句。

Fill in the blanks with the following words and make sentences.

例句：[妈妈] 是 [老师]，[爸爸] 也是 [老师]。

1. 先生　夫人　经理
2. 先生　小姐　美国人
3. 哥哥　姐姐　学生
4. 经理　秘书　日本人

[　　]是[　　]，
[　　]也是[　　]。

例句：妈妈 是 老师，爸爸 不是 老师。

1. 爸爸　哥哥　经理
2. 姐姐　妹妹　秘书
3. 先生　小姐　俄罗斯
4. 安娜　杰克　法国

☐是，☐

☐不是☐。

四、把下面的词组成句子。

Rearrange the following words into sentences.

1. 我　你　认识　高兴　很
2. 也　我　你　很　认识　高兴
3. 经理　我　是　不
4. 吗　小姐　中国人　是

五、快速回答。

Give quick responses to the following questions.

1. 谁认识经理？
2. 经理是中国人吗？
3. 你高兴吗？
4. 我很高兴，你呢？
5. 他很高兴，你呢？

六、写课内生词并注拼音。

Copy the new words of the text and give the *pinyin* of each word.

3

第三课　我的朋友

Lesson 3　My Friends

学拼音

The Phonetic Alphabet (III)

一、韵母 Vowels

ua　uo　uai　uei (ui)　uan　un　uang　ueng

üe　üan　ün

1. 拼读练习 Combine sounds into syllables.

	ua	uo	uai	ui	uan	un	uang	ueng
d		duo		dui	duan	dun		
t		tuo		tui	tuan	tun		
n		nuo			nuan			
l		luo			luan	lun		
z		zuo		zui	zuan	zun		
c		cuo		cui	cuan	cun		
s		suo		sui	suan	sun		
zh	zhua	zhuo	zhuai	zhui	zhuan	zhun	zhuang	
ch	chua	chuo	chuai	chui	chuan	chun	chuang	
sh	shua	shuo	shuai	shui	shuan	shun	shuang	
r	rua	ruo		rui	ruan	run		
g	gua	guo	guai	gui	guan	gun	guang	
k	kua	kuo	kuai	kui	kuan	kun	kuang	
h	hua	huo	huai	hui	huan	hun	huang	

	ü	üe	üan	ün
d				
t				
n	nü	nüe		
l	lü	lüe		
j	ju	jue	juan	jun
q	qu	que	quan	qun
x	xu	xue	xuan	xun

2. 辨音练习 Distinguish the sounds.

duo—tuo	dui—tui	duan—tuan	dun—tun
ku—gu	kuai—guai	kun—gun	kuang—guang
hu—hua	hai—huai	hei—hui	han—huan
jue—que	juan—quan	jun—qun	xie—xue
zhu—chu	chu—shu	zhua—shua	zhui—chui
zhai—zhuai	zhan—zhuan	zhen—zhun	zhang—zhuang
chai—chuai	chan—chuan	che—chun	chang—chuang
shai—shuai	shan—shuan	shen—shun	shang—shuang

二、声调 Tones

声调练习 Practice the tones.

xuē xué xuě xuè
xiāo xiáo xiǎo xiào } xuéxiào (school)

jiāo jiáo jiǎo jiào
shī shí shǐ shì } jiàoshì (classroom)

shuī shuí shuǐ shuì
guō guó guǒ guò } shuǐguǒ (fruit)

qī qí qǐ qì
chuāng chuáng chuǎng chuàng } qǐ chuáng (to get up)

xī xí xǐ xì
zāo záo zǎo zào } xǐ zǎo (to take a bath)

ānquán (safety)
cānguān (to visit)
fāngfǎ (method)
hépíng (peace)
kāi xué (school begins)
nénglì (ability)
qiāo mén (to knock at the door)
shuì jiào (to sleep)
wǔhuì (ball, dancing party)
yǐnliào (beverage)
bàozhǐ (newspaper)
diànhuà (telephone)
guānzhào (to look after)
jiějué (to solve)
lìrùn (profit)
péitóng (to accompany)
rénmín (people)
tóngzhì (comrade)
xiūxi (to rest)
zhuōzi (table)

课 文
Text

1. A: 嗨，安娜，你 认识 山口 吗？
Hēi, Ānnà, nǐ rènshi Shānkǒu ma?

B: 谁 是 山口？
Shéi shì Shānkǒu?

A: 我 的 日本 朋友。
Wǒ de Rìběn péngyou.

B: 对不起，我 不 认识。
Duìbuqǐ, wǒ bú rènshi.

2. A: 谢 文，那 是 谁？
Xiè Wén, nà shì shéi?

B: 山口。
Shānkǒu.

A: 她 是 留学生 吗？
Tā shì liúxuéshēng ma?

B: 是。我们 是 同学。
Shì. Wǒmen shì tóngxué.

A: 你们 是 朋友 吗？
Nǐmen shì péngyou ma?

B: 我们 是 好 朋友！
Wǒmen shì hǎo péngyou!

3. A: 嗨，山口！
Hēi, Shānkǒu!

C: 嗨，谢 文！
Hēi, Xiè Wén!

A: 山口，我 介绍 一下，这 是 安娜，我 的 朋友。
Shānkǒu, wǒ jièshào yíxià, zhè shì Ānnà, wǒ de péngyou.

C: 是 你的 女朋友 吗？
Shì nǐ de nǚpéngyou ma?

A: 安娜，你 说 呢？
Ānnà, nǐ shuō ne?

B: 不，我 不 是 他 的 女朋友！
Bù, wǒ bú shì tā de nǚpéngyou!

生词 New Words

1. 的	de	*used after an attribute, indicating possession, connection or relation*
2. 朋友	péngyou	friend
3. 那	nà	that
4. 留学生	liúxuéshēng	foreign student
5. 们	men	*used after a personal pronoun or a noun referring to a person to form a plural*

6. 同学	tóngxué	schoolmate, fellow student; *a form of address used when speaking to a student*
7. 介绍	jièshào	to introduce; introduction
8. 一下	yíxià	*used after a verb to indicate an action or a try*
9. 女	nǚ	female, woman, girl, daughter
10. 说	shuō	to speak, to talk, to say

专名 Proper Noun

山口	Shānkǒu	Yamaguchi

注释 Notes

1 元音i单独成音节时，要写成yi，在一个音节开头时，要写成y。例如：

The vowel i, when it is a syllable by itself, is written as yi. When it is at the beginning of a syllable, it is written as y. For example:

i—yi	yìdiǎnr（a little），yìbiān（one side）
ie—ye	yě shì（also），yèwǎn（night）
ia—ya	yáchǐ（tooth），yàjūn（runner-up）
iao—yao	yāoqǐng（to invite），yàojǐn（important）

in、ing 自成音节时，要写成 yin、ying。如 Yīngyǔ（English）。

When in or ing stands alone as a syllable, they should be written as yin or ying respectively, e.g., Yīngyǔ (English).

2 元音 u 单独成音节时，要写成 wu，在一个音节的开头时，要写成 w。例如：

The vowel u, when it is a syllable by itself, is written as wu. When it is at the beginning of a syllable, it is written as w. For example:

u—wu　　wūzi（room），wùhuì（to misunderstand）
uo—wo　　wǒmen（we, us），wòpù（sleeping berth）
uan—wan　　wánxiào（joke），wǎn'ān（good night）

3　元音 ü 在单独成音节或在一个音节开头时，要写成 yu；在 ü 及 ü 开头的韵母和声母 j、q、x 相拼时，ü 上的两点要省去。例如：

The vowel ü, when it is a syllable by itself, or when it is at the beginning of one syllable, is written as yu. When ü or other compound vowels beginning with ü are combined with j, q or x, the two dots of ü should be omitted. For example:

ü—yu　　Hànyǔ（Chinese），yúkuài（joyful）
üan—yuan　　yuǎnjìn（far and near），yuànyì（willing）
jü—ju　　jūzhù（to live），júzi（tangerine）
qü—qu　　jiāoqū（suburb），qùnián（last year）
xü—xu　　xūyào（need），xǔduō（many）

4　“的”，助词，用在定语和中心语之间，表示修饰或限定关系，例如：

的 is a particle placed between the attribute and the headword to express a modifying or determining relationship. For example:

谁的书　　我的朋友　　她的老师　　谢文的同学
经理的秘书　　爸爸的弟弟　　很好的朋友

5　“一下”，用在动词后面，表示做一次或试着做；也表示短暂的时间。例如：

一下 is used after a verb, indicating doing something once or trying to do something. It also expresses a very short time. For example:

说一下　　介绍一下　　认识一下

补充生词 Additional New Words

1. 男　　nán　　man, son, boy, male

2. 太太　　tàitai　　Mrs., Madame, wife
3. 爱人　　àiren　　husband, wife, lover
4. 同事　　tóngshì　　colleague
5. 书　　shū　　book

练习 Exercises

一、替换练习。
Substitution drills.

A：山口，你认识杰克吗？
B：杰克是谁？
A：杰克是我的美国朋友。
B：对不起，我不认识。

安娜	谢文	法国
杰克	朱丽亚	俄罗斯
谢文	山口	日本

A：嗨，我介绍一下，这是谢文。
B：你的朋友？
A：是，谢文是我的朋友。
B：他是美国人吗？
A：不，他不是美国人。

安娜	同事	俄罗斯
朱丽亚	秘书	法国
山口	经理	日本
杰克	老师	英国

二、给下列句子标注拼音，然后朗读，注意语调。
Give the *pinyin* of the following sentences, and then read them aloud, paying special attention to the intonation.

谁？　　　　他是谁？
你的朋友　　他是我的中国朋友。
我的朋友　　他是你的中国朋友？

三、把下面的词组成句子。

Rearrange the following words into sentences.

1. 他　朋友　的　是　我
2. 我　留学生　是　美国
3. 他　杰克　认识　朋友　的
4. 介绍　你　朋友　的　一下

四、为下列单词写拼音并组句熟读。

Write the *pinyin* of the following words, make sentences with them, and read them repeatedly.

1. 他——是——我——爸爸

   我们——是——好——朋友
2. 我——认识——爸爸——的——同事

   爸爸——的——同事——也——认识——我
3. 爸爸——的——同事——介绍——他——的——女——朋友

   他——的——女——朋友——介绍——爸爸——的——同事

模仿上面的例句，把下面的词组成句子，看谁组成的句子多，然后反复朗读。

Make sentences with the following words by imitating the examples given above. See who can make the largest number of sentences and then read them repeatedly.

同学	认识	的	爸爸	我
同事	介绍		妈妈	你
朋友	是		哥哥	他
经理			姐姐	
秘书			弟弟	
			妹妹	
			安娜	
			杰克	
			谢文	

五、会话练习。

Situational conversations.

情景 1：两个不认识的人第一次见面。

Scene 1: Two strangers meet for the first time.

情景 2：三个人第一次见面，其中两个人是互相认识的朋友。

Scene 2: Three people meet for the first time, but two of them are friends who have already known each other.

六、写课内生词并注拼音。

Copy the new words of the text and give the *pinyin* of each word.

4

第四课　怎么称呼
Lesson 4　How to Address a Person

学拼音
The Phonetic Alphabet（IV）

一、辨音练习 Distinguish the sounds.

b—p　zhēn bàng—zhēn pàng（very good indeed—very fat indeed）
bái bān—pái bān（day shift—to arrange shifts）
bèidòng—péitóng（passive—to accompany）
biànyī—piányi（plain clothes—cheap）

d—t　dāpèi—tā péi（collocation—He'll pay for it.）
dàijià—tài jiǎ（price—too phoney）
dānxīn—tàn qīn（to worry—to visit one's relatives）
dǐxì—tǐxì（ins and outs—system）

g—k　gǎi dào—kāi dào（to change the course—to clear the way）
gānjìng—kànqīng（clean—to see clearly）
gàojǐng—kàojìn（to give an alarm—to draw near）
guàiyì—kuàiyì（weird—pleased）

j—q　dǎ jiǔ—dǎ qiú（to buy wine—to play a ball game）
jiājiào—qiàqiǎo（family education—by chance）
jīngjì—qīnqi（economy—relative）
jìjié—qīnqiè（season—kind）

z—c zǎ zhǎo—cā zǎo (how to find it—to take a sponge bath)
zāiqíng—cáiqíng (condition of a disaster—talent)
zào yáo—cǎoyào (to start a rumor—herbal medicine)
zuòguài—cuòguài (to do mischief—to blame sb. wrongly)

r—n ráotou—náotóu (extra—to scratch one's head)
ránliào—nán liào (fuel—difficult to expect)
réncái—nèn cài (talented person—tender vegetables)
rìqī—nìjì (date—to go into hiding)

二、声调练习 Practice the tones.

bàngōngshì (office) bīngjīlíng (ice cream)
Jiànlìbǎo (Jianlibao) túshūguǎn (library)
zìxíngchē (bicycle)
nào xiàohua (to make a fool of oneself)
niàn shēngcí (to read the new words)
xiě Hànzì (to write Chinese characters)
tīng lùyīn (to listen to the recording)
zuò liànxí (to do exercises)
cháyú-fànhòu (over a cup of tea or after a meal—at one's leisure)
Kěkǒu Kělè (Coca-Cola)
fùxí kèwén (to review the text)
yùxí shēngcí (to preview the new words)
Hàn-Yīng cídiǎn (Chinese-English dictionary)
Jīng Mào Dàxué (University of International Business and Economics)
shēngyi xīnglóng (Business is booming.)
cáiyuán màoshèng (to be rich in financial resources)

课文
Text

1. A: 你 姓 什么？
Nǐ xìng shénme?
B: 我 姓 万。
Wǒ xìng Wàn。
A: 叫 什么 名字？
Jiào shénme míngzi?
B: 文杰。 万 文杰。
Wénjié. Wàn Wénjié.

2. A: 请进！
Qǐngjìn!
B: 你 是 高 先生 吗？
Nǐ shì Gāo xiānsheng ma?
A: 我 是 高 亚安，您 怎么 称呼？
Wǒ shì Gāo Yà'ān, nín zěnme chēnghu?
B: 我 姓 万， 叫 万 文杰。
Wǒ xìng Wàn, jiào Wàn Wénjié.
A: 啊， 万 先生， 请 坐！
À, Wàn xiānsheng, qǐng zuò!
B: 谢谢！
Xièxie!

3. A: 请问， 您 贵姓？
Qǐngwèn, nín guìxìng?
B: 免 贵 姓 万， 万 文杰。
Miǎn guì xìng Wàn, Wàn Wénjié.
A: 啊，是 万 先生， 幸会！
À, shì Wàn xiānsheng, xìnghuì!

B: 幸会!
Xìnghuì!

生 词
New Words

1. 怎么	zěnme	how, why
2. 称呼	chēnghu	to call, to address
3. 姓	xìng	surname, family name
4. 什么	shénme	what
5. 叫	jiào	to name, to call
6. 名字	míngzi	name
7. 请	qǐng	please, to request, to invite
8. 进	jìn	to enter, to come in / into
9. 坐	zuò	to sit
10. 问	wèn	to ask, to inquire
11. 您	nín	(*honorific*) you
12. 贵姓	guìxìng	(*honorific*) your surname
13. 免	miǎn	to dismiss, to dispense, to avoid
14. 幸会	xìnghuì	very pleased to meet you

专 名 Proper Nouns

1. 万文杰	Wàn Wénjié	Wan Wenjie
2. 高亚安	Gāo Yà'ān	Gao Ya'an

注 释
Notes

1 现代汉语普通话的声调，除四个基本声调和轻声外，有些字连读时，还会出现声调变化，学习时要用心掌握和多练习。

Apart from the four basic tones and the neutral tone, the tones of characters in modern Chinese may vary when words are read together. This requires special attention and repeated practice.

1. 两个或几个第三声连读字，除最后一个字读原调外，前面的字都要读成二声，书写时仍标原调号。例如：

When two or several characters in the third tone are read together, while the last character retains the original third tone, the others are changed into the second tone. But the original tone mark is kept in the phonetic spelling. For example:

Nǐ hǎo. → Ní hǎo.　　　Wǒ hěn hǎo. → Wó hén hǎo.

2. 第三声的字在其他三个声调字和绝大部分轻声字前面时，要念成半三声，调值为 (21)，例如：

Characters in the third tone, when occurring before characters in the other three tones or most neutral tones, are pronounced as the first half of the third tone, the tone pitch being (21). For example:

Nǐ hǎo ma?
qǐngwèn
hěn máng
hǎo、qǐng、hěn 都只读前一半降调。

hǎo, qǐng and hěn in the above examples are all read as the first half of the third tone, which is actually falling.

3. “不”字单用或在第一、二、三声字前读第四声。例如：

When the character 不 is used by itself, or when it is used before characters in the first, second or third tones, it is pronounced in the fourth tone. For example：

bù gāi (shouldn’t)　　bù néng (can’t)　　bù hǎo (not good)

在第四声字前读第二声。如：

When it is used before characters in the fourth tone, it is pronounced in the second tone. For example：

bù huì → bú huì
bù qù → bú qù
bù shì → bú shì

2 “您”和“你”，都是第二人称代词。“您”是敬称，比较客气，多用来称呼长者或第一次见面的同辈。如果是很熟悉的同事或很好的朋友，用“您”称呼对方，反而显得太客气了，用“你”倒更合适一些。

您 and 你 are both second personal pronouns. 您 is honorific, which is more polite, and usually used to address a senior person or someone who one meets for the first time. Between well-acquainted colleagues or good friends, 您 sounds too polite for addressing the other party. In these circumstances, 你 is more appropriate.

3 “贵姓”，在询问对方姓名时，为了表示尊敬与礼貌，常说“您贵姓？”对方回答时为了表示客气，常说“免贵”。询问男性的名字用“大名”，询问女性的名字用“芳名”，也是一种客气的询问方式。

贵姓 (honorable surname) is used to show respect and politeness, and 您贵姓 is often used to ask the other person's name. In reply, the other person would say 免贵. Also for the sake of politeness, 大名 (formal name) is used to ask a man's name, while 芳名 (good name) is used to ask a lady's name.

补充生词 Additional New Words

1. 芳名	fāngmíng	name of a young girl
2. 大名	dàmíng	(*honorific*) your name, formal name
3. 久仰	jiǔyǎng	I have long been looking forward to meeting you.

练习 Exercises

一、替换练习。

Substitution drills.

A：你姓什么？
B：我姓关。
A：你叫什么名字？
B：我叫关亚东。

朱	朱同文
安	安小朋
谢	谢贵友

A：请问，您贵姓？
B：我姓安。
A：怎么称呼？
B：我的中国名字叫安小朋。
A：你是留学生吗？
B：是。我是法国留学生。

谢	谢贵友	俄罗斯
朱	朱丽亚	美国
韩	韩绍芳	英国

A：请问，你的经理是谁？
B：他姓万，叫万文杰。
A：万文杰？我认识他。
B：你认识我的经理，我很高兴。

秘书	朱	朱丽亚
老师	高	高文英

二、把下面的词组成句子。

Rearrange the following words into sentences.

1. 他　什么　名字　叫
2. 你　经理　称呼　怎么　的
3. 好　是　朋友　他们
4. 名字　你　是　谢贵友　吗　的　叫

三、完成对话。

Complete the following dialogues.

A：你是万先生吗？
B：________，________。您怎么称呼？
A：________________。
B：很高兴认识你。
A：________________。

A：请问，您贵姓？

B：________，________。

A：久仰，久仰。

B：你是……

A：我是________。

B：幸会，幸会。

四、用下列动词短语各组两个句子。

Make two sentences with each of the following verb phrases.

例句：你去请一下老师。

1. 介绍一下
2. 问一下
3. 认识一下

五、会话练习。

Situational conversations.

情景 1：你去拜访一位你还不认识的人。

Scene 1: You go and visit someone you don't know.

情景 2：两个不认识的人初次见面，彼此问候并询问对方情况。

Scene 2: Two strangers meet for the first time, greeting and inquiring about each other.

六、写课内生词并注拼音。

Copy the new words of the text and give the *pinyin* of each word.

5

第五课　打电话

Lesson 5　Making Telephone Calls

课　文

Text

1. A: 喂，你 好！
   Wèi, nǐ hǎo!

   B: 你 好！ 请问， 谢 太太 在 吗？
   Nǐ hǎo! Qǐngwèn, Xiè tàitai zài ma?

   A: 你 打错 电话 了！
   Nǐ dǎcuò diànhuà le!

   B: 对不起！
   Duìbuqǐ!

2. A: 喂，您 好！这 是 爱友 公司。
   Wèi, nín hǎo! Zhè shì Àiyǒu Gōngsī.

   B: 你 好！ 请问， 高 亚安 先生 在 吗？
   Nǐ hǎo! Qǐngwèn, Gāo Yà'ān xiānsheng zài ma?

   A: 他 不 在。您 有 什么 事 吗？
   Tā bú zài. Nín yǒu shénme shì ma?

   B: 啊，请 他 回来 后 给 我 打 个 电话。
   À, qǐng tā huílái hòu gěi wǒ dǎ gè diànhuà.

   A: 您 的 电话 号码 是……
   Nín de diànhuà hàomǎ shì…

B: 68370641。
68370641.

A: 好 的，再见！
Hǎo de, zàijiàn!

3. A: 喂，是 68370641 吗？
Wèi, shì 68370641 ma?

B: 是，我 是 万 文杰。
Shì, wǒ shì Wàn Wénjié.

A: 你 好。我 是 高 亚安。
Nǐ hǎo. Wǒ shì Gāo Yà'ān.

B: 我 给 你 打 电话，你 不 在。
Wǒ gěi nǐ dǎ diànhuà, nǐ bú zài.

A: 你 有 什么 事 吗？
Nǐ yǒu shénme shì ma?

B: 你 知道 谢 太太 的 电话 吗？
Nǐ zhīdào Xiè tàitai de diànhuà ma?

A: 知道，64960057。
Zhīdào, 64960057.

B: 好，谢谢！
Hǎo, xièxie!

生词 New Words

1. 打	dǎ	to make (a call), to strike, to play
2. 电话	diànhuà	telephone
3. 喂	wèi	hello, hey
4. 在	zài	*a preposition indicating time, place, situation, scope, etc.*
5. 错	cuò	wrong; fault

6. 公司	gōngsī	company, corporation
7. 有	yǒu	to have, to possess; there be
8. 事	shì	thing, matter, affair
9. 回来	huílái	to return, to come back
10. 后	hòu	after
11. 给	gěi	to give
12. 号码	hàomǎ	number
13. 一（1）	yī	one
14. 二（2）	èr	two
15. 三（3）	sān	three
16. 四（4）	sì	four
17. 五（5）	wǔ	five
18. 六（6）	liù	six
19. 七（7）	qī	seven
20. 八（8）	bā	eight
21. 九（9）	jiǔ	nine
22. 十（10）	shí	ten
23. 零（0）	líng	zero
24. 再见	zàijiàn	goodbye, bye
25. 知道	zhīdào	to know, to realize, to be aware of

注　释
Notes

1　“在”，动词，表示人或事物的存在，后边跟的宾语是存在的处所、位置。“在”的宾语常省略。否定形式是在动词“在”的前面加副词“不”。例如：

在, a verb, expresses the existence of a person or thing. The object that follows it indicates the place or location. Its object is often omitted. The negative form of 在 is to add the adverb 不 before the verb 在. For example:

A：高先生在吗？
B：高先生不在。

A：高先生在家吗？
B：他不在家。

经理办公室在315。
他的宿舍在407。

2 "给"，介词。介词不能单独使用，它后面必须跟名词、代词或词组构成介词结构，一起在句子中充当定语、状语、补语。例如：

给 is used as a preposition, which cannot be used alone. It must be followed by a noun, pronoun or phrase to form a prepositional structure to function as an attribute, adverbial or complement in a sentence. For example:

1. 请给我打电话！
2. 给我介绍一下。

3 现代汉语的句子成分：汉语的句子，一般都有主语、谓语、宾语三个基本成分和附加修饰成分。主语和宾语前面可以有定语，定语是修饰和限定主语和宾语的。谓语前面可以有状语，状语表示谓语的情态、程度、范围、时间、处所等；谓语后面可以有补语，补充说明谓语的结果、程度、时间、处所、数量等。汉语句子成分的排列顺序如下：

（定语）主语→〔状语〕谓语〈补语〉→（定语）宾语

符号表示：

主：══	谓：──
宾：～～	定：（ ）
状：〔 〕	补：〈 〉

The sentence elements in modern Chinese: A Chinese sentence generally contains three basic elements (subject, predicate, and object), and other supplementary modifying elements. Preceding the subject and object, there may be the attribute, which is used to modify or determine the subject and object. Preceding the predicate, there can be the adverbial, which tells the manner, degree, scope, time, or place of the predicate. Following the predicate, there can be the complement, which explains the result, degree, time, place, or quantity of the predicate. The sequence of the Chinese sentence elements can be shown as follows:

(Attribute) Subject→〔Adverbial〕Predicate〈Complement〉→(Attribute) Object

They can also be indicated by the following signs：

Subject：══　　Predicate：——

Object：～～　　Attribute：（ ）

Adverbial：〔 〕　　Complement：〈 〉

例如：

For example:

1. 我　叫　杰克。
2. 我　认识　（他的）　老师。
3. （他的）妹妹　是　（我的）　朋友。
4. 我们　认识　〈一下〉。
5. 我　〔很高兴〕　认识　（你的）　同事。

补充生词 Additional New Words

1. 转	zhuǎn	to pass on, to transfer, to turn
2. 占线	zhànxiàn	The line is busy.
3. 办公室	bàngōngshì	office
4. 宿舍	sùshè	dormitory, hostel
5. 教室	jiàoshì	classroom
6. 手机	shǒujī	mobile phone
7. 留言	liúyán	to leave a message
8. 发	fā	to send, to deliver
9. 短信	duǎnxìn	short message, text message

练习
Exercises

一、替换练习。
Substitution drills.

A：你好！请问山口小姐在吗？
B：她不在，你是谁？
A：我是她的朋友，叫高亚安。
B：请问，你有什么事吗？
A：请她回来后给我打个电话。
B：好的。

万经理	杰克
安秘书	朱丽亚
朱老师	谢文

A：喂，请问，高亚安在吗？
B：高亚安，你的电话！
A：高亚安吗？我是谢文。
C：你好，谢文，有什么事吗？
A：你知道山口办公室的电话吗？
C：知道。64947362。
A：好，谢谢。

安娜	朱丽亚	杰克宿舍	64938754
万文杰	安娜	老师办公室	64967235
杰克安	亚娜	万经理公司	68479601

二、把下面的词组成句子。
Rearrange the following words into sentences.

1. 你　谁　电话　给　打
2. 我　不　手机　她　号码　知道　的
3. 你　电话　请问　的　号码　多少　是
4. 打　你　了　错　电话
5. 请　办公室　我　电话　给　打

三、完成对话。

Complete the following dialogues.

A：你知道山口宿舍的电话号码吗？
B：__________，__________。

A：请问，万经理在吗？
B：__________，__________。

A：安小姐不在吗？请她回来后给我打个电话。
B：__________。

A：经理不在，您有什么事吗？
B：__________。

四、根据下面的数字山读出各种组合，练习自己的发音。

Practice pronunciation by forming combinations of the figures given in the following triangle.

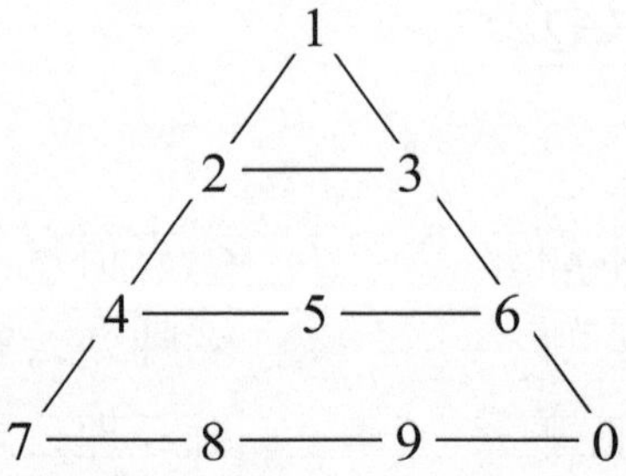

五、换词组句练习（三句以上）。

Replace the underlined words in the following sentences to make more than three new sentences for each one.

1. 请你给我打电话。
2. 经理在办公室吗？

六、把下面的词或词组扩展成句子。

Expand the following words and phrases into sentences.

1. 电话
打电话
请打电话

2. 事
什么事
有什么事

3. 号码
电话号码
你的电话号码

4. 短信
发短信
发什么短信

七、会话练习。

Situational conversations.

情景 1：A 给 B 打电话，开始电话没人接，后来电话占线，最后电话通了。

Scene 1: A is calling B. At first, nobody answers, then the line is busy. Finally he gets through.

情景 2：B 给 A 打电话，A 不在办公室，B 给 A 的手机留言。

Scene 2: B is calling A. A is not in the office. B leaves a text message on A’s mobile phone.

八、朗读《普通话声韵拼合总表》。

Read aloud the Table of the Combinations of the Initials and Finals in *Putonghua*.

6

第六课　预订房间
Lesson 6　Booking a Room

课　文
Text

1. A: 您　好！这　是　北京　饭店　服务台。
   Nín hǎo! Zhè shì Běijīng Fàndiàn fúwùtái.

   B: 你好！我　要　预订　一个　房间。
   Nǐ hǎo! Wǒ yào yùdìng yí gè fángjiān.

   A: 要　套间　吗？
   Yào tàojiān ma?

   B: 不，标准间。
   Bù, biāozhǔnjiān.

   A: 什么　时候　来？
   Shénme shíhou lái?

   B: 明天。
   Míngtiān.

   A: 请问　先生　贵姓？
   Qǐngwèn xiānsheng guìxìng?

   B: 我　姓　王。
   Wǒ xìng Wáng.

   A: 恭候　您的　光临！
   Gōnghòu nín de guānglín!

2. A：小姐，我 要 一 个 房间。
Xiǎojie, wǒ yào yí gè fángjiān.

B：您 预订 了 吗？
Nín yùdìng le ma?

A：昨天 我 打 电话 预订 了。
Zuótiān wǒ dǎ diànhuà yùdìng le.

B：请问 先生 贵姓？
Qǐngwèn xiānsheng guìxìng?

A：我 姓 王。
Wǒ xìng Wáng.

B：请 稍 等。3702 房间，可以 吗？
Qǐng shāo děng. 3702 fángjiān, kěyǐ ma?

A：可以，谢谢！
Kěyǐ, xièxie!

B：别 客气！
Bié kèqi!

生词 New Words

1. 预订 yùdìng to book, to subscribe; reservation
2. 房间 fángjiān room
3. 服务台 fúwùtái service desk, reception desk
4. 要 yào to want, to ask for
5. 个 gè *a general measure word*
6. 套间 tàojiān suite
7. 标准间 biāozhǔnjiān standard room
8. 时候 shíhou time, moment
9. 来 lái to come
10. 明天 míngtiān tomorrow
11. 恭候 gōnghòu to await respectfully

12. 光临	guānglín	to honor sb. with one's presence
13. 了	le	*a particle indicating the completion of an action or a change*
14. 昨天	zuótiān	yesterday
15. 稍	shāo	a bit, a little
16. 等	děng	to wait, to await
17. 可以	kěyǐ	can, may
18. 别	bié	don't, had better not
19. 客气	kèqi	polite, courteous

专　名　Proper Nouns

1. 北京饭店	Běijīng Fàndiàn	Beijing Hotel
2. 王	Wáng	Wang (a surname)

注　释
Notes

1　"要"，动词，表示希望得到或保持什么。例如：

要, as a verb, expresses that one wants something or wants to keep something. For example:

1. 我要一本书。
2. 他要标准间。
3. 他要你的电话号码。

"要"，也是助动词，放在动词或形容词前，表示做某件事的意志。例如：

要 is also an auxiliary verb, used before a verb or an adjective to express the will to do something. For example:

1. 她要换钱。
2. 经理要预订一个房间。
3. 我要好好谢谢老师。

2 “个”，量词。汉语里有大量量词，能够计量的人或事物，都有特定的量词，这是在长期的社会交际活动中形成的，是一种“习惯用法”，不可乱用。量词的使用，是外国朋友学习中的一个难点，学习时要特别注意。下面是量词“个”的常用例子：

个 is a measure word. There are many measure words in Chinese. Each of the persons or things to be measured goes with a specific measure word. These have resulted from social communications over the years and become set expressions which cannot be changed randomly. The use of measure words is the crux for foreign Chinese learners and merits special attention in their studies. What follows are some common examples of the use of the measure word 个:

一个人	三个宿舍
一个教师	四个弟弟
一个教室	一个晚上
一个房间	十个学生

3 “了”，助词，附在动词后边，表示动作已经完成。例如：

了, a particle, is used after a verb to indicate that the action has been completed. For example:

1. 他来了。
2. 他预订了一个房间。
3. 杰克今天换了钱。
4. 我刚才给她打了电话。

补充生词
Additional New Words

1. 今天	jīntiān	today
2. 前天	qiántiān	the day before yesterday
3. 后天	hòutiān	the day after tomorrow
4. 单人间	dānrénjiān	single room
5. 双人间	shuāngrénjiān	double room

练习 Exercises

一、替换练习。
Substitution drills.

A：小姐，可以预订房间吗？
B：可以。请问先生贵姓？
A：我姓谢。
B：先生要什么房间？
A：一个单人间。

万	双人间
朱	套间
安	标准间

A：小姐，我要一个房间。
B：您预订了吗？
A：我昨天预订了。
B：先生贵姓？
A：我姓谢。
B：请稍等。7023号房间，可以吗？
A：可以。

前天	万	1409
昨天下午	安	5678
今天上午	朱	3642

A：先生，这是您的房间。
B：啊，不错。
A：有什么事，请打电话。
服务台的电话是0109。
B：谢谢！
A：别客气！

小姐	很好	4001
夫人	太好了	2323

二、把下面的词组成句子。
Rearrange the following words into sentences.

1. 饭店　吗　服务台　是
2. 王秘书　我　预订　给　房间　一个

3. 你　打　预订　可以　电话　房间
4. 先生　时候　饭店　来　什么

三、完成对话。

Complete the following dialogues.

A：请问，可以预订房间吗？
B：________________________。

A：你预订的房间好吗？
B：________________________。

A：在你的房间可以打电话吗？
B：________________________。

A：北京饭店的服务好吗？
B：________________________。

四、组词练习。

Make phrases.

打____　知道____　认识____
问____　介绍____　预订____
等____　____台

五、扩展句子，然后熟读。

Expand the following into sentences, and then read them repeatedly.

1. 房间
单人房间
一个单人房间

2. 等
等你
等你来

六、会话练习。

Situational conversations.

情景：打电话预订房间（标准间，单人间，双人间，套间）。

Scene: Book a room by phone (a standard room, a single room, a double room, a suite).

七、给下面的拼音标上调号，然后朗读几遍。

Mark the tones of the following *pinyin* and then read aloud the passage for several times.

Wang xiansheng gei Beijing Fandian da dianhua, ta shuo, ta yao yuding yi ge fangjian, shi yi ge biaozhunjian. Beijing Fandian fuwutai de xiaojie wen ta: "Shenme shihou lai fandian?" Wang xiansheng shuo: "Mingtian." Fuwutai de xiaojie shuo: "Gonghou nin de guanglin!"

7

第七课　换钱

Lesson 7　Changing Money

课　文

Text

1. A：小姐，我们 要 换 钱。
Xiǎojie, wǒmen yào huàn qián.

B：是 现金 还是 旅行 支票？
Shì xiànjīn háishi lǚxíng zhīpiào?

A：是 现金。
Shì xiànjīn.

C：我 的 是 旅行 支票。
Wǒ de shì lǚxíng zhīpiào.

B：你们 要 换 多少？
Nǐmen yào huàn duōshao?

A：今天 的 汇率 是 多少？
Jīntiān de huìlǜ shì duōshao?

B：100 美元 兑换 689.80 人民币。
100 měiyuán duìhuàn 689.80 rénmínbì.

A：好 的，我 换 500 美元。你 换 不 换？
Hǎo de, wǒ huàn 500 měiyuán. Nǐ huàn bu huàn?

C：我 不 换 了。
Wǒ bú huàn le.

2. A: 小姐，我 刚才 换了 500 美元 的 人民币。
Xiǎojie, wǒ gāngcái huànle 500 měiyuán de rénmínbì.

B: 有 什么 问题 吗？
Yǒu shénme wèntí ma?

A: 今天 100 美元 兑换 689.80 人民币，对 吗？
Jīntiān 100 měiyuán duìhuàn 689.80 rénmínbì, duì ma?

B: 对！
Duì!

A: 500 美元 换 3459？
500 měiyuán huàn 3459?

B: 先生， 是 3449，不 是 3459。
Xiānsheng, shì 3449, bú shì 3459.

A: 哦，是 我 算错 了，对不起。
Ò, shì wǒ suàncuò le, duìbuqǐ.

B: 没 关系。
Méi guānxi.

生词 New Words

1. 换	huàn	to change, to exchange
2. 钱	qián	money
3. 现金	xiànjīn	cash
4. 还是	háishi	or, still, yet
5. 旅行	lǚxíng	travel, tour, journey
6. 支票	zhīpiào	cheque
7. 多少	duōshao	how many, how much
8. 汇率	huìlǜ	exchange rate
9. 美元	měiyuán	U.S. dollar

10. 兑换	duìhuàn	to exchange, to convert
11. 元（块）	yuán (kuài)	*yuan* (*kuai*)
12. 角（毛）	jiǎo (máo)	*jiao* (*mao*) (*fraction unit of Chinese currency equal to 1/10 of a yuan*)
13. 人民币	rénmínbì	Renminbi
14. 刚才	gāngcái	a moment ago, just now
15. 问题	wèntí	question, problem, issue
16. 哦	ò	oh
17. 算	suàn	to calculate, to compute, to figure

注　释
Notes

1　“还是”，连词，用在选择疑问句中。选择疑问句，是句子中并列列出两项或多项情况，要求选择其中一项回答的句子。例如：

还是, as a conjunction, is used in an alternative question to select one answer from two or more alternatives listed in the sentence. For example:

A：是现金还是旅行支票？
B：是现金。

A：你今天晚上来还是不来？
B：我今天晚上来。

A：你要单人间还是双人间？
B：我要双人间。

2　“换不换？”这是一种正反疑问句。正反疑问句，是用谓语的肯定+否定形式表示疑问的句子，即“谓语+不（没）+谓语”。这种疑问句，要做出肯定或否定的明确回答。例如：

换不换? is a positive-negative question. It is formed by the positive form of the predicate plus the negative form of the predicate, i.e., “predicate+不(or 没) +

predicate". This kind of question requires a definite positive or negative answer. For example:

A：你认识不认识安娜？
B：我认识。

A：你们经理好不好？
B：不好！

A：他高兴不高兴？
B：他很不高兴！

补充生词 Additional New Words

1. 银行	yínháng	bank
2. 分	fēn	*fen (a fraction unit of Chinese currency equal to 1/100 of a yuan)*
3. 百（100）	bǎi (yìbǎi)	hundred
4. 千（1000）	qiān (yìqiān)	thousand
5. 万（10000）	wàn (yíwàn)	ten thousand
6. 点	diǎn	point, dot, drop
7. 英镑	yīngbàng	pound sterling
8. 日元	rìyuán	Japanese yen
9. 港币	gǎngbì	Hong Kong dollar
10. 欧元	ōuyuán	Euro

练 习
Exercises

一、替换练习。
Substitution drills.

A：你有钱吗？
B：有。
A：有多少？
B：有38元。

50元	100元
120元	290元
336元	891元

A：小姐，我要换钱。
B：现金还是旅行支票？
A：现金。

美元	英镑
日元	欧元
美元	日元

A：小姐，今天的汇率是多少？
B：您是问美元兑换人民币的汇率吗？
A：是的。
B：100美元兑换689.80元人民币。

日元	6.009元
英镑	838.58元
港币	88.983元

二、完成对话。
Complete the following dialogues.

A：小姐，我要换钱。
B：______________________？

A：你是美国人还是英国人？
B：我是 ____________________。

A：____________________还是____________________？
B：我是中国学生。

A：你今天换不换钱？
B：不，________________。

A：你有什么事？
B：我要 ________________。

三、给下面的词语配上适当的动词，然后扩展成句子。

Add a verb to each of the following words, then expand them into sentences.

______朋友　　　　　　　______钱
______房间　　　　　　　______电话

四、完成句子。

Complete the following sentences.

1. ______介绍还是不介绍？
2. ______等还是不等？
3. ______打电话还是不打电话？
4. ______预订还是不预订？

五、将下列正反疑问句改成一般问句，然后做出回答。

Turn the following positive-negative questions into general questions, and then answer them.

例句：你打不打电话？ → 你打电话吗？

1. 你等不等你的朋友？
2. 先生预订不预订房间？
3. 他要不要现金？
4. 你换不换钱？
5. 经理问不问他的秘书？

六、快速读出下面的钱数。

Read the following figures quickly.

1.50 元	1 元 2 角 3 分	643 元人民币
1.23 元	3 元 5 角 8 分	18456 元人民币
4.10 元	10 元 4 角 5 分	197274 元人民币
11.37 元	21 元零 8 分	

七、会话练习。

Situational conversation.

情景：一个美国留学生在银行服务台换钱。

Scene: An American student is changing money at the counter of a bank.

八、阅读下面的一段话，然后用拼音把这段话写出来。

Read the following passage, and then write it in *pinyin*.

今天，一个留学生在银行换钱。他换了钱，算了算，说："啊，不对，银行少给了我十元钱。""小姐，你少给了我十元钱！"小姐说："您刚才换了五百美元，我给了您三千四百四十九元，您再算算！"他说："啊，是我算错了，对不起！"

8

第八课　出租车

Lesson 8　Taxi

课　文

Text

1. A：出租车！

Chūzūchē!

B：先生，请上车！您去哪儿？

Xiānsheng，qǐng shàng chē! Nín qù nǎr?

A：去北京饭店。

Qù Běijīng Fàndiàn.

B：请坐好！

Qǐng zuòhǎo!

A：到友谊商店的时候，请停一下车。

Dào Yǒuyì Shāngdiàn de shíhou，qǐng tíng yíxià chē.

B：好的。

Hǎo de.

2. B：先生是来旅行的吗？

Xiānsheng shì lái lǚxíng de ma?

A：不。我是来做生意的。

Bù. Wǒ shì lái zuò shēngyi de.

B：您刚到北京吧？

Nín gāng dào Běijīng ba?

A: 是。你 怎么 知道?
Shì. Nǐ zěnme zhīdào?

B: 我 是 出租车 司机!
Wǒ shì chūzūchē sījī!

A: 到 友谊 商店 了?
Dào Yǒuyì Shāngdiàn le?

B: 没有 到,堵车 了!
Méiyǒu dào, dǔchē le!

A: 哦!
Ò!

3. B: 先生, 北京 饭店 到 了。
Xiānsheng, Běijīng Fàndiàn dào le.

A: 多少 钱?
Duōshao qián?

B: 48 块。
48 kuài.

A: 这 是 50 块。
Zhè shì 50 kuài.

B: 找 您 两 块。
Zhǎo nín liǎng kuài.

A: 请 给 我 发票!
Qǐng gěi wǒ fāpiào!

B: 好 的。
Hǎo de.

A: 谢谢!
Xièxie!

B: 再见!
Zàijiàn!

生 词
New Words

1. 出租车	chūzūchē	taxi
2. 上车	shàng chē	to get on a vehicle
3. 去	qù	to go
4. 哪儿	nǎr	where
5. 到	dào	to arrive, to reach
6. 停车	tíngchē	to stop, to pull up, to park
7. 做	zuò	to do, to make, to carry on
8. 生意	shēngyi	business, trade
9. 刚	gāng	just, exactly
10. 吧	ba	*a particle used at the end of a sentence, indicating mood*
11. 司机	sījī	driver
12. 没有	méiyǒu	not to have, there is not, to be without
13. 堵车	dǔchē	to be jammed with traffic
14. 找	zhǎo	to give change, to look for
15. 发票	fāpiào	receipt, invoice

专 名 Proper Noun

友谊商店	Yǒuyì Shāngdiàn	Friendship Store

注 释
Notes

1 “是……的”，这是一个常用的句式。“是……的”中间一般是动词、状动短语或主谓短语。当某一动作已经在过去发生，而要强调动作发生的时间、处所、方式、条件、目的、对象、工具等，就可以用这种句式。例如：

是……的 is a commonly used sentence pattern usually with a verb, adverbial-verb phrase or subject-predicate phrase in the middle. It is used to emphasize the time, place, way, condition, purpose, object, or tool and so on of an action which has occurred. For example:

1. 他是昨天来的。
2. 这是在中国买的。
3. 他是来旅行的。
4. 杰克是坐飞机来的。

2 “刚”“刚才”，表示行为、事件等在说话前不久发生。“刚”是副词，只能用在动词前，“刚才”是名词。试比较下面的句子：

刚 or 刚才 is used to indicate that a certain action or thing took place not long before the statement. 刚 is an adverb used only before a veb and 刚才 is a noun. Compare the following sentences:

1. 他刚认识安娜。
2. 朱丽亚刚来中国。
3. 刚才他在这儿。
4. 刚才的考试很难。

3 “吧”，语气助词，常用在句子末尾。

吧 is a modal particle. It is usually used at the end of a sentence.

1. 表示命令、请求、催促、建议等。

It can be used to indicate a command, a request, an urge, or a suggestion.

1）请坐吧！
2）你去吧！
3）请他明天来吧！

2. 表示疑问。这种句子，常表示一种估计、推测的语气。

It can be used to express doubt, often with a mood of estimation or guessing.

1）你刚到北京吧？
2）你不认识他吧？
3）那是王老师吧？

3. 表示同意。

It can also be used to express agreement.

1）好吧！

2）可以吧！

3）来吧！

补充生词 Additional New Words

1. 打的	dǎdī	to take a taxi
2. 公里	gōnglǐ	kilometer
3. 起价	qǐjià	minimum charge, starting price
4. 下车	xià chē	to get off
5. 开车	kāichē	to drive
6. 系	jì	to tie, to fasten
7. 安全带	ānquándài	safety belt
8. 邮局	yóujú	post office

练习 Exercises

一、替换练习。

Substitution drills.

A：先生，您去哪儿？

B：我去友谊商店。

商店　　银行

邮局　　服务台

办公室

A：小姐是来留学的吗？

B：不，我是来旅行的。

学习汉语　　做生意

旅行　　学习

预订房间　　坐出租车

找经理　　找秘书

A：这是你的车吗？
B：不，这是饭店的。

房间	安娜
钱	我爸
办公室	经理
司机	杰克

二、把下面的词组成句子。
Rearrange the following words into sentences.

1. 我　邮局　去　要
2. 哪儿　车　可以　停
3. 请　叫　我　给　出租车
4. 你　打的　北京饭店　可以　去

三、完成对话。
Complete the following dialogues.

A：你知道在中国怎么打的吗？
B：________________________。

A：你坐出租车要发票吗？
B：________________________。

A：你来北京做什么？
B：________________________。

A：在北京开车，要系安全带吗？
B：________________________。

四、为下列词语配上合适的动词。
Add appropriate verbs to the following words.

______生意　　______钱　　______旅行
______安全带　　______房间　　______车
______经理　　______服务台

五、为下列句子选用“刚”或“刚才”，并把它放在合适的位置。

Add 刚 or 刚才 to the following sentences in the appropriate positions.

1. 经理下车了。
2. 你去哪儿了？
3. 他要发票了。
4. 秘书预订房间。
5. 堵车了。
6. 他做生意。
7. 我的男朋友认识我的父亲。
8. 司机去银行了。

六、读下列句子，注意句中的“是……的”。

Read the following sentences and pay attention to 是……的 in them.

1. 我是开车的。
2. 钱是我给的。
3. 他是我介绍的。
4. 他是昨天来的。
5. 这是爸爸给我的。
6. 他是来做生意的。

七、会话练习。

Situational conversation.

情景：钱太太要去银行换钱，叫出租车。到了银行，司机停车等她换钱。换钱后，钱太太去饭店看朋友。

Scene: Mrs. Qian is going to change money at the bank. She calls a taxi and gets to the bank. The driver waits for her while she is changing money. Then she goes to a hotel to see her friend.

八、给下面的拼音标上调号，然后朗读几遍。

Mark the tones of *pinyin* in the following passage and then read it for several times.

Yi ge Meiguoren gang dao Beijing, zuo chuzuche qu Beijing Fandian. Ta yao chuzuche siji dao Youyi Shangdian de shihou ting yixia che. Che ting le, ta wen: “Dao Youyi Shangdian le?” Siji shuo: “Meiyou dao, du che le!” “O, zaotou le!” (It’s too bad!)

9

第九课　他没来上班

Lesson 9　He Has Not Turned up for Work

课　文
Text

1. A: 小　王，给我　准备　车。
Xiǎo Wáng, gěi wǒ zhǔnbèi chē.

B: 什么　时候　要？
Shénme shíhou yào?

A: 半　个　小时　以后。
Bàn ge xiǎoshí yǐhòu.

B: 好　的。
Hǎo de.

2. A: 喂，　张　师傅　在　吗？
Wèi, Zhāng shīfu zài ma?

B: 他　不　在。
Tā bú zài.

A: 他　去　哪儿　了？
Tā qù nǎr le?

B: 他　没　来　上班。
Tā méi lái shàngbān.

A: 哦，谢谢！
Ò, xièxie!

3. A: 您 好！这 是 饭店 总 服务台。
Nín hǎo! Zhè shì fàndiàn zǒng fúwùtái.

B: 你 好！我 是 爱友 公司。我们 要 一 辆 车。
Nǐ hǎo! Wǒ shì Àiyǒu Gōngsī. Wǒmen yào yí liàng chē.

A: 什么 时候 用？
Shénme shíhou yòng?

B: 九 点 四十五 分。
Jiǔ diǎn sìshíwǔ fēn.

A: 就 是 一 刻钟 以后，对 吧？
Jiù shì yí kèzhōng yǐhòu, duì ba?

B: 对！ 行 吗？
Duì! Xíng ma?

A: 没 问题。
Méi wèntí.

B: 谢谢！
Xièxie!

4. A: 经理，车 已经 安排 好 了。
Jīnglǐ, chē yǐjīng ānpái hǎo le.

B: 谢谢！
Xièxie!

A: 一 刻钟 以后 在 饭店 门口 上 车。
Yí kèzhōng yǐhòu zài fàndiàn ménkǒu shàng chē.

B: 是 张 师傅 开 车 吗？
Shì Zhāng shīfu kāi chē ma?

A: 不 是。张 师傅 今天 没 上班，是 饭店 的 车。
Bú shì. Zhāng shīfu jīntiān méi shàngbān, shì fàndiàn de chē.

B: 好，知道 了。
Hǎo, zhīdào le.

生 词
New Words

1. 上班	shàngbān	to go to work, to be on duty
2. 准备	zhǔnbèi	to prepare, to get ready
3. 半	bàn	half
4. 小时	xiǎoshí	hour
5. 以后	yǐhòu	after, afterwards, later
6. 师傅	shīfu	(*a polite address for skilled men*) master
7. 总	zǒng	general, overall, total
8. 辆	liàng	*a measure word for vehicles*
9. 用	yòng	to use, to employ
10. 点	diǎn	point, o'clock
11. 分	fēn	minute
12. 就	jiù	exactly, precisely
13. 刻	kè	quarter (of an hour)
14. 钟	zhōng	bell, clock, time (as measured in hours and minutes)
15. 行	xíng	to be all right, will do
16. 已经	yǐjīng	already
17. 安排	ānpái	to arrange
18. 门口	ménkǒu	entrance, doorway, gate

注 释
Notes

1 “不”“没有”，都是副词，表示否定。“没有”用于对动作完成的否定或对事物性质变化的否定，后面不能带“了”，所以不能用于将来时态。试比较“不”和“没有”的用法：

Both 不 and 没有 are adverbs indicating negation. 没有 is used to negate the completion of an action or the change of the nature of a certain object. So it can neither take 了 after it, nor be used with a future time. Compare the usage between 不 and 没有.

1. 他今天不来了。（这是回答“他今天来不来？”）
2. 他今天没有来。（这是回答“他今天来没来？”）
3. 他昨天来了吗?
4. 他昨天也没来。（不能回答“他昨天也不来。”）
5. 他明天来吗?
6. 他明天也不来。（不能回答“他明天也没来。”）

“没”“没有”，也是动词。“有”表示领有、占有。“没有”是“有”的否定词。例如：

没 and 没有 can be used as verbs too. 有 means possessing or owning. 没有 is the negation of 有. For example：

1. 他有钱。
2. 我没有钱。
3. 他有秘书。
4. 我没有秘书。

2 “已经”，副词，表示动作完成或达到了某种程度。它修饰的动词或形容词，句子后边一般要带“了”。例如：

已经, an adverb, expresses that an action is done or has reached a certain extent. It usually modifies a verb or an adjective and is usually followed by 了 at the end of a sentence. For example:

1. 他已经大了。
2. 车已经停了。
3. 我们已经认识了。
4. 她已经下班了。
5. 现在已经九点了。
6. 他已经高兴起来了。

补充生词
Additional New Words

1. 下班	xiàbān	to get off work
2. 过	guò	to exceed; beyond, past
3. 差	chà	to be less than, to be short of
4. 整	zhěng	full, entire, exactly
5. 现在	xiànzài	now, present

练　习
Exercises

一、替换练习。
Substitution drills.

A：现在几点了？
B：现在<u>八点</u>了。

7:40	8:15
9:30	9:45
10:10	11:55
12:05	22:00

A：你们几点<u>上班</u>？
B：我们<u>八点上班</u>。

下课	11:45
下班	下午 6:00
上课	上午 10:10

二、把下面的词组成句子。
Rearrange the following words into sentences.

1. 经理　已经　好　车　准备　了　的
2. 我们　哪儿　在　上车
3. 请　饭店　在　上车　门口
4. 今天　谁　是　开车
5. 爸爸　下班　今天　6:45

三、完成对话。

Complete the following dialogues.

A：你什么时候上班，什么时候下班？
B：________________________________。

A：现在你有事吗？
B：________________________________。

A：一刻钟以后，在饭店门口上车，可以吗？
B：________________________________。

A：去旅行，你要准备什么？
B：________________________________。

A：你明天不来上班吗？
B：________________________________。

四、用下面的词说时间。

Use the following words to talk about time.

正　差　过　零　刻　半

现在是______________________。

0:00	0:05	1:00	3:10
4:15	5:30	7:45	8:45
12:55	12:00	13:03	16:30
20:08	21:15	23:50	

五、用"不"或"没有"填空，然后做出回答。

Fill in the blanks with 不 or 没有, and then answer the questions.

1. 张师傅今天______来上班吗？
2. 秘书昨天______预订房间吗？

3. 今天______安排吗？

4. 你______发票吗？

六、会话练习。

Situational conversation.

情景：给饭店总服务台或出租车公司打电话要一辆车。

Scene: Call the general service desk of a hotel or a taxi company for a taxi.

七、阅读下面的一段话，然后用拼音把这段话写出来。

Read the following passage and then write it in *pinyin*.

经理要秘书小王安排一辆车。一刻钟以后，小王给经理打电话，说车已经安排好了，请经理一刻钟以后在饭店大门口上车。经理问："是张师傅开车吗？"小王说："张师傅没有来上班，是饭店的车。"经理说："知道了。"

10

第十课　今天是她的生日

Lesson 10　It Is Her Birthday Today

课　文

Text

1. A: 啊，好　漂亮　的　鲜花！

   À,　hǎo piàoliang de xiānhuā!

   B: 给　您！

   Gěi nín!

   A: 送　给我？小　王，你……

   Sòng gěi wǒ? Xiǎo Wáng, nǐ…

   B: 这　是　我　替　您　买　的。

   Zhè shì wǒ　tì　nín mǎi de.

   A: 我　没　叫　你　买　花啊！

   Wǒ méi jiào nǐ　mǎi huā　a!

   （电话　响了，B 接　电话。）

   (Diànhuà xiǎngle, B　jiē diànhuà.)

   B: 喂，噢，是　钱　太太。他　在，您　等等。经理，您　的　电话。

   Wèi, ō,　shì Qián tàitai.　Tā　zài, nín děngdeng. Jīnglǐ, nín de diànhuà.

2. A: 喂，亲爱的，有事吗？
Wèi, qīn'ài de, yǒu shì ma?

B: 现在 几 点 了？
Xiànzài jǐ diǎn le?

A: 现在 六 点。
Xiànzài liù diǎn.

B: 你 还 不 回 家？
Nǐ hái bù huí jiā?

A: 啊，对不起，晚上 我 还 有 一 个 约会。
À, duìbuqǐ, wǎnshang wǒ hái yǒu yí gè yuēhuì.

B: 你 忘了 今天 是 什么 日子？
Nǐ wàngle jīntiān shì shénme rìzi?

A: 十 月 三十 日，星期 五。
Shí yuè sānshí rì, xīngqī wǔ.

B: 谁 问 你 这个 了！
Shéi wèn nǐ zhège le!

3. A: 小 王，我 太太 刚才 打 电话，好像 很 生气。
Xiǎo Wáng, wǒ tàitai gāngcái dǎ diànhuà, hǎoxiàng hěn shēngqì.

B: 为 什么？
Wèi shénme?

A: 她 问 我，今天 是 什么 日子。
Tā wèn wǒ, jīntiān shì shénme rìzi.

B: 您 怎么 说？
Nín zěnme shuō?

A: 我 说，今天 是 十 月 三十 日，星期 五。
Wǒ shuō, jīntiān shì shí yuè sānshí rì, xīngqī wǔ.

B: 您 太太 就 挂 电话 了？
Nín tàitai jiù guà diànhuà le?

A: 是。我 说错 日子 了？
Shì. Wǒ shuōcuò rìzi le?

B: 没错。
Méi cuò.

A: 她为什么生气呢？
Tā wèi shénme shēngqì ne?

B: 今天是您太太的生日，我的大经理！
Jīntiān shì nín tàitai de shēngrì, wǒ de dà jīnglǐ!

A: 哦，天哪！谢谢你替我买的鲜花！快给我取消晚上的约会。
Ò, tiān na! Xièxie nǐ tì wǒ mǎi de xiānhuā! Kuài gěi wǒ qǔxiāo wǎnshang de yuēhuì.

生词 New Words

1. 生日	shēngrì	birthday
2. 漂亮	piàoliang	beautiful, pretty, good-looking
3. 鲜花	xiānhuā	(fresh) flowers
4. 送	sòng	to deliver, to give
5. 替	tì	to take the place of; for
6. 买	mǎi	to buy, to purchase
7. 亲爱的	qīn'ài de	dear
8. 还	hái	still, also; in addition (*expressing discovery or emphasis*)
9. 回	huí	to return, to go back, to reply
10. 家	jiā	home
11. 约会	yuēhuì	appointment
12. 忘	wàng	to forget
13. 日子	rìzi	date, day
14. 月	yuè	month, moon
15. 日	rì	day, sun
16. 星期	xīngqī	week

17. 好像	hǎoxiàng	to seem, to be like
18. 生气	shēngqì	to get angry, to take offense
19. 为什么	wèi shénme	why
20. 挂	guà	to hang up (the phone), to put up
21. 大	dà	big, large, great
22. 天	tiān	sky, day
23. 哪	na	*a particle used after a word ending with* n *to indicate exclamation or suggestion*
24. 快	kuài	quick, fast, soon
25. 取消	qǔxiāo	to cancel, to abolish

注释 Notes

1 “好”，副词，放在动词或形容词前，强调程度，意思和“多么”差不多，表达一种感叹语气。例如：

好, as an adverb, is placed before a verb or an adjective to emphasize the degree. Its meaning is similar to 多么, expressing an exclamatory mood. For example:

1. 这花好漂亮！
2. 她好高兴啊！
3. 秘书小姐好客气啊！
4. 他太太好生气啊！

2 “还”，副词，表示行为、动作或某种情况维持不变。例如：

还, as an adverb, indicates that a behavior, an action, or a certain situation remains unchanged. For example:

1. 他们还没下班。
2. 他还生我的气呢！
3. 他还没有女朋友。
4. 我还没有给她打电话。

"还"，还可以表示在某种程度或范围以外有所增加或补充。例如：

还 also expresses addition or supplement beyond a certain degree or scope. For example:

1. 他有一个中国朋友，还有一个美国朋友。
2. 昨天，我见到了钱经理，还见到了他的太太。
3. 钱经理买了鲜花，还买了生日蛋糕。

3 "就"，副词，说明时间。当两件事先后连续发生，在说明后一件事的句子中用"就"字时，表示后一件事紧接着前一件事发生。例如：

就 is an adverb indicating time. When two events happen one after the other, 就 is used before the second event, indicating that it happens right after the first one. For example:

1. 刚到五点钟，他就回家了。
2. 老板进门就叫秘书去买花。
3. 他见了老师就问问题。
4. 我有了钱就去旅行。

补充生词 Additional New Words

1. 星期一	xīngqī yī	Monday
2. 星期二	xīngqī èr	Tuesday
3. 星期三	xīngqī sān	Wednesday
4. 星期四	xīngqī sì	Thursday
5. 星期五	xīngqī wǔ	Friday
6. 星期六	xīngqī liù	Saturday
7. 星期日（星期天）	xīngqīrì (xīngqītiān)	Sunday
8. 周末	zhōumò	weekend
9. 上星期	shàng xīngqī	last week
10. 下星期	xià xīngqī	next week
11. 年	nián	year
12. 蛋糕	dàngāo	cake

练习
Exercises

一、替换练习。
Substitution drills.

A：你的生日是什么时候？
B：5月15日是我的生日。

你弟弟	8月25日	我弟弟
你爸爸	1月1日	我爸爸
你妈妈	7月30日	我妈妈
你女朋友	5月16日	我女朋友

A：星期五晚上，你有约会吗？
B：没有。星期六晚上我有一个约会。

今天	明天
星期一	星期三
星期二	星期五
星期六	星期日

A：你去哪儿？
B：我回家。

学校	宿舍
教室	办公室

A：你送她什么？
B：我送她鲜花。

生日蛋糕	一本书
一些钱	一辆车

二、把下面的词组成句子。
Rearrange the following words into sentences.

1. 晚上　你　吗　约会　有
2. 她　约会　了　取消
3. 今天　生日　是　的　我
4. 请　电话　挂　你　别
5. 你　我　替　老师　问问　吧

三、朗读下面的会话，然后替换画线部分的词语再朗读。

Read aloud the following dialogues, and then replace the underlined parts and read them aloud again.

A：啊，经理，今天您好漂亮！
B：谢谢。你知道为什么吗？
A：我知道，今天是您的生日。

A：经理，刚才您太太来电话了。
B：有什么事吗？
A：她谢谢您送给她鲜花。
B：我没送给她鲜花啊？
A：是我替您买的。
B：为什么？
A：您忘了，今天是您太太生日！
B：哦，谢谢你！

四、完成对话。

Complete the following dialogues.

A：你知道你父母的生日吗？
B：________________。

A：你父母的生日你送鲜花吗？
B：________________。

A：你为什么给你的朋友打电话？
B：________________。

A：她为什么生你的气？
B：________________。

A：你找经理什么事？

B：______________________。

五、指出下列句子中“还”的不同用法。

Point out how 还 is used in the following sentences.

1. 什么时候了，你还没有预订房间？
2. 我问了谢小姐，还问了高先生。
3. 他找错了钱，还不说对不起。
4. 经理周末还工作。
5. 你还有什么事吗？

六、用下列词语和副词“就”造句。

Make sentences with the following expressions and the adverb 就 .

1. 买了鲜花　回家
2. 有钱　买车
3. 到了　打电话
4. 做错事　生气
5. 去银行　换钱

七、会话练习。

Situational conversations.

情景 1：打电话，为朋友预订生日蛋糕。

Scene 1: Make a phone call to order a birthday cake for your friend.

情景 2：给朋友送生日蛋糕和鲜花。

Scene 2: Give the birthday cake and flowers to your friend.

八、给下面的拼音标上调号，然后朗读几遍。

Mark the tones of *pinyin* in the following passage and then read it aloud for several times.

Jintian, shi Qian taitai de shengri. Qian taitai gei Qian jingli da dianhua, wen ta shenme shihou hui jia. Qian jingli shuo, ta wanshang hai you yuehui, yao hen wan cai hui jia. Qian taitai hen shengqi, yixia jiu guale dianhua. Qian jingli wen mishu Xiao Wang, ta zuocuo shenme shi le, Xiao Wang shuo: "Wo de da jingli, jintian shi nin taitai de shengri!" Qian jingli shuo: "O, wo zenme wang le!"

11

第十一课　你想做什么（一）

Lesson 11　What Do You Want to Do (I)

课　文

Text

在课上　Zài Kè Shang

王　老师：同学们，　你们 大家 都 认识 了 吧？
Wáng lǎoshī: Tóngxuémen, nǐmen dàjiā dōu rènshi le ba?

杰克：　我 先 介绍 一下 我 自己。
Jiékè: Wǒ xiān jièshào yíxià wǒ zìjǐ.

山口：　不 用 介绍，我 知道 你 叫 杰克，美国人。
Shānkǒu: Bú yòng jièshào, wǒ zhīdào nǐ jiào Jiékè, Měiguórén.

杰克：　我 也 知道 你 叫 山口，日本人。
Jiékè: Wǒ yě zhīdào nǐ jiào Shānkǒu, Rìběnrén.

珍妮：　我们 互相 都 认识。
Zhēnnī: Wǒmen hùxiāng dōu rènshi.

山口：　我 还 知道，珍妮 来 中国 学习 汉语。
Shānkǒu: Wǒ hái zhīdào, Zhēnnī lái Zhōngguó xuéxí Hànyǔ.

珍妮：　可是，你 知道 我 为 什么 学习 汉语 吗？
Zhēnnī: Kěshì, nǐ zhīdào wǒ wèi shénme xuéxí Hànyǔ ma?

山口：　那 还 用 问？为了 以后 在 中国 做 生意！
Shānkǒu: Nà hái yòng wèn? Wèile yǐhòu zài Zhōngguó zuò shēngyi!

珍妮：　对！也 不对！
Zhēnnī: Duì! Yě búduì!

杰克：这 是 什么 意思？
Jiékè: Zhè shì shénme yìsi?
珍妮：杰克，我 问 你，你 为 什么 学习 汉语？
Zhēnnī: Jiékè, wǒ wèn nǐ, nǐ wèi shénme xuéxí Hànyǔ?
杰克：我 喜欢 交 朋友。
Jiékè: Wǒ xǐhuan jiāo péngyou.
珍妮：山口，你 呢？
Zhēnnī: Shānkǒu, nǐ ne?
山口：我？我 爱 玩儿。不 学 汉语，怎么 在 中国 旅行？
Shānkǒu: Wǒ? Wǒ ài wánr. Bù xué Hànyǔ, zěnme zài Zhōngguó lǚxíng?

王 老师：同学们，你们 刚才 都 说 认识 珍妮，对 吧？
Wáng lǎoshī: Tóngxuémen, nǐmen gāngcái dōu shuō rènshi Zhēnnī, duì ba?
杰克：是。我们 都 认识 珍妮。
Jiékè: Shì. Wǒmen dōu rènshi Zhēnnī.
王 老师：你们 了解 珍妮 吗？
Wáng lǎoshī: Nǐmen liǎojiě Zhēnnī ma?
山口：还 不 太 了解。
Shānkǒu: Hái bú tài liǎojiě.
珍妮：我们 互相 都 还不太 了解。
Zhēnnī: Wǒmen hùxiāng dōu hái bú tài liǎojiě.
山口：珍妮 刚才 说 的 话，我 和 杰克 就 不 太 明白。
Shānkǒu: Zhēnnī gāngcái shuō de huà, wǒ hé Jiékè jiù bú tài míngbai.
王 老师：珍妮，你 学习 汉语 不是 为了 做 生意 吗？
Wáng lǎoshī: Zhēnnī, nǐ xuéxí Hànyǔ bú shì wèile zuò shēngyi ma?
珍妮：当 服务员 也 是 在 做 生意。
Zhēnnī: Dāng fúwùyuán yě shì zài zuò shēngyi.

杰克：你不想当服务员？
Jiékè: Nǐ bù xiǎng dāng fúwùyuán?

珍妮：不想当！
Zhēnnī: Bù xiǎng dāng!

山口：当秘书？
Shānkǒu: Dāng mìshū?

珍妮：不！
Zhēnnī: Bù!

杰克：那你想做什么？
Jiékè: Nà nǐ xiǎng zuò shénme?

生词 New Words

1. 想	xiǎng	to think, to want, would like to
2. 大家	dàjiā	all, everybody
3. 都	dōu	all, even
4. 先	xiān	earlier, at first
5. 自己	zìjǐ	oneself
6. 互相	hùxiāng	mutually, each other
7. 学习	xuéxí	to study, to learn
8. 可是	kěshì	but, yet, however
9. 为了	wèile	for, in order to, for the sake of
10. 意思	yìsi	to mean
11. 喜欢	xǐhuan	to like, to love
12. 交	jiāo	to associate with (friends), to make (friends)
13. 爱	ài	to love
14. 玩儿	wánr	to play, to have fun
15. 了解	liǎojiě	to understand, to acquaint oneself with
16. 太	tài	too, very

17. 话	huà	word, talk
18. 和	hé	and
19. 明白	míngbai	clear, obvious
20. 当	dāng	to work as, to serve as, to be
21. 服务员	fúwùyuán	waiter, waitress, attendant
22. 那（么）	nà (me)	then, in that case

专 名 Proper Noun

汉语	Hànyǔ	Chinese

注 释 Notes

1 "用"，动词，意思是使用、利用工具、手段做事或实现某种目的。例如：

用, as a verb, indicates the use or utilization of a tool or a means to do something or to achieve a certain aim. For example:

1. 他用车送儿子上学。
2. 这是用姐姐的钱买的鲜花。
3. 他用旅行支票换现金。

"用"，也可以表示"需要"，多用否定形式"不用"或反问形式"还用"，就是不需要的意思。例如：

用 also means "need", and is often used in the negative form 不用 or rhetorical form 还用, meaning "no need". For example:

1. 今天是星期天，不用上班。
2. 不用问，她就是你的女朋友！
3. 不用打电话，我自己去找他。
4. 那还用说？

2 “在”，介词，跟表处所的名词或词组组成介词短语，在句子中做定语、状语或补语。例如：

在, a preposition, forms a prepositional phrase with a noun or an expression of place, which functions as an attribute, an adverbial, or a complement. For example:

1. 小王在一家公司上班。
2. 在北京的留学生都交了中国朋友。
3. 出租车停在饭店的门口。

“在”或“正在”，还是时间副词，表示行为、动作处在进行的状态。例如：

在 or 正在 is a temporal adverb, indicating that the action or motion is in progress. For example:

1. 我们在上课，不要说话。
2. 爸爸上班的时候，我在学习汉语。
3. 他进来的时候，我正在打电话。
4. 我正在上班，你自己去买花吧！

补充生词 Additional New Words

1. 英语	Yīngyǔ	English
2. 法语	Fǎyǔ	French
3. 日语	Rìyǔ	Japanese
4. 以前	yǐqián	before, previously

练习 Exercises

一、替换练习。
Substitution drills.

A：你想做什么？
B：我想做生意。

玩儿去	旅行
当老师	当银行经理

A：你喜欢什么？
B：我喜欢旅行。

开车玩儿	学习汉语
朋友送我鲜花	交中国朋友

A：你在做什么？
B：我正在学习。

工作	打电话
学习开车	想她说的话

二、把下面的词组成句子。
Rearrange the following words into sentences.

1. 你　汉语　为什么　学习
2. 我们　大家　她　都　喜欢
3. 这　自己　我　是　事　的
4. 我　她　了解　不　还
5. 我　明白　你　话　不　说　的

三、朗读下面的会话，然后替换画线部分的词语，再朗读。
Read aloud the following dialogues, and then replace the underlined parts and read them aloud again.

A：同学们，你们互相都认识了吧？
B：是，我们不用自我介绍了。
A：你们为什么来中国？
B：为了学习汉语。

A：你喜欢学习汉语吗？
B：还可以。
A：你这是什么意思？
B：就是这个意思。
A：我不太明白。
B：还可以就是还可以。

四、完成对话。

Complete the following dialogues.

A：你为什么学习汉语？
B：________________________。

A：你了解你的中国朋友吗？
B：________________________。

A：你喜欢交什么朋友？
B：________________________。

A：请问，你喜欢做什么？
B：________________________。

五、把下面的词组扩展成句子。

Expand the following phrases into sentences.

1. 互相学习
2. 互相了解
3. 互相打电话
4. 互相约会
5. 互相问问题

六、完成句子。

Complete the following sentences.

1. 以前他在__________________。
   现在他在__________________。

2. 他以前用汉语__________________。
   他现在用英语__________________。

3. 以前经理上班请司机__________________。
   现在经理不用司机__________________。

4. 不用客气，你不明白的话，可以__________________。

5. 他刚学习汉语，__________________。

七、请介绍你喜欢什么，不喜欢什么。

Talk about your likes and dislikes.

八、会话练习。

Situational conversation.

情景：A 与 B 互相问对方想做什么。

Scene: A and B ask each other about what they want to do.

九、阅读下面的一段话，然后用拼音把这段话写出来。

Read the following passage and then write it in *pinyin*.

同学们正在上课，老师想知道他们是不是都互相认识了。同学们说，都认识了，可是还不太了解。比如（bǐrú for example），大家学好汉语以后都想做什么呢？杰克说，他学好汉语是为了交朋友；山口说，她学好汉语是为了在中国旅行；珍妮想做什么呢？珍妮说了，可大家还是不明白。

12

第十二课 你想做什么（二）

Lesson 12 What Do You Want to Do (II)

课 文

Text

在课外 Zài Kè Wài

服务员： 欢迎！ 欢迎！ 请 进！
Fúwùyuán: Huānyíng! Huānyíng! Qǐng jìn!

刘 经理： 王 老师，您 好！
Liú jīnglǐ: Wáng lǎoshī, nín hǎo!

王 老师：你 是……
Wáng lǎoshī: Nǐ shì…

刘 经理： 王 老师 不 认识 我 了？ 我 是 您 的 学生 刘 亮 啊！
Liú jīnglǐ: Wáng lǎoshī bú rènshi wǒ le? Wǒ shì nín de xuésheng Liú Liàng a!

王 老师：是 你 啊，刘 亮！ 你 也 是 来 玩儿 的 吗？
Wáng lǎoshī: Shì nǐ ā, Liú Liàng! Nǐ yě shì lái wánr de ma?

刘 经理： 不。我 是 这个 酒吧 的 经理。
Liú jīnglǐ: Bù. Wǒ shì zhège jiǔbā de jīnglǐ.

王 老师：哦？ 我 记得，你 刚 工作 三 年，就 当 经理 了？
Wáng lǎoshī: Ó? Wǒ jìde, nǐ gāng gōngzuò sān nián, jiù dāng jīnglǐ le?

刘经理：　老师　忘　了，我　是　学　经济　管理　的。
Liú jīnglǐ:　Lǎoshī wàng le,　wǒ shì xué jīngjì guǎnlǐ de.

王　老师：啊，对，你　还　很　努力，学　得　很　不错！
Wáng lǎoshī: À,　duì,　nǐ hái hěn nǔlì,　xué de hěn búcuò!

刘经理：　王　老师，你们　喝　点儿　什么？　别　客气！
Liú jīnglǐ:　Wáng lǎoshī, nǐmen hē diǎnr shénme? Bié kèqi!

王　老师：随便，茶、可口　可乐、橙汁，　都　可以。
Wáng lǎoshī: Suíbiàn, chá, Kěkǒu Kělè, chéngzhī, dōu kěyǐ.

杰克：　我　要　啤酒。
Jiékè:　Wǒ yào píjiǔ.

刘经理：　好　的。服务员！
Liú jīnglǐ:　Hǎo de. Fúwùyuán!

珍妮：　刘　先生，你　刚　工作　三　年　就　当　经理
　了，是　真　的？
Zhēnnī:　Liú xiānsheng, nǐ gāng gōngzuò sān nián jiù dāng jīnglǐ
　le,　shì zhēn de?

刘经理：　是　真　的。
Liú jīnglǐ:　Shì zhēn de.

杰克：　珍妮，你　也　想　当　酒吧　经理？
Jiékè:　Zhēnnī, nǐ yě xiǎng dāng jiǔbā jīnglǐ?

珍妮：　怎么，　不行　啊？我　还　想　当　老板、
　总裁　呢！
Zhēnnī:　Zěnme, bùxíng a?　Wǒ hái xiǎng dāng lǎobǎn,
　zǒngcái ne!

杰克：　行，　当然　行！不过……
Jiékè:　Xíng, dāngrán xíng! Búguò…

珍妮：　不过　什么？
Zhēnnī:　Búguò shénme?

杰克：　你　得　先　到　这儿　来　当　服务员！
Jiékè:　Nǐ děi xiān dào zhèr lái dāng fúwùyuán!

珍妮：　为　什么？
Zhēnnī:　Wèi shénme?

杰克：　先　学　走，再　学　跑　啊！
Jiékè:　Xiān xué zǒu, zài xué pǎo a!

山口：　　珍妮 不学 走也会 跑！哈……
Shānkǒu:　　Zhēnnī bù xué zǒu yě huì pǎo! Hā…

生词 New Words

1. 欢迎	huānyíng	to welcome
2. 酒吧	jiǔbā	bar
3. 记得	jìde	to remember
4. 工作	gōngzuò	to work; job
5. 经济	jīngjì	economy
6. 管理	guǎnlǐ	to manage; management
7. 努力	nǔlì	to make great efforts, to exert oneself
8. 得	de	*a particle used after a verb or an adjective to introduce a complement of result or degree*
9. 喝	hē	to drink
10. 随便	suíbiàn	whatever, random, any
11. 茶	chá	tea
12. 橙汁（儿）	chéngzhī (r)	orange juice
13. 啤酒	píjiǔ	beer
14. 真	zhēn	true, real, indeed
15. 老板	lǎobǎn	boss
16. 总裁	zǒngcái	whatever CEO, president
17. 当然	dāngrán	of course
18. 不过	búguò	but
19. 得	děi	*an auxiliary verb expressing a volitional or factual necessity*
20. 这儿	zhèr	here
21. 走	zǒu	to walk

22. 会　huì　can, to be able to, to be good at
23. 跑　pǎo　to run
24. 哈　hā　ha

专　名　Proper Nouns

1. 刘亮　Liú Liàng　Liu Liang
2. 可口可乐　Kěkǒu Kělè　Coca-Cola

注　释
Notes

1　"得"（de），结构助词，用在动词或形容词的后边，连接表示结果或程度的补语。例如：

得 (de) is a structural particle used after a verb or an adjective to link up a complement of result or degree. For example:

1. 你的汉语说得真好。
2. 他的生意做得很不错。
3. 他们玩儿得很高兴。
4. 这个酒吧管理得太好了。
5. 安娜高兴得说个不停。

2　"得"（děi），助动词，口语里常用，表示意志上或事实上的必要。例如：

得 (děi) is an auxiliary verb which is often used in spoken Chinese to express a volitional or factual necessity. For example:

1. 我得好好谢谢你。
2. 你得多练习。
3. 现在八点钟了，我得去上班了。
4. 开车的时候，得系好安全带。

注意："得"的否定形式是"不用"，不说"不得"。例如：

Note: The negative form of 得 is 不用, but we don't use 不得. For example:

1. 她得工作。
   她不用工作。

2. 今天得学习。
   今天不用学习。

补充生词 Additional New Words

1. 咖啡	kāfēi	coffee
2. 矿泉水	kuàngquánshuǐ	mineral water
3. 饮料	yǐnliào	beverage, drink
4. 酒	jiǔ	alcoholic drink, wine, liquor
5. 葡萄酒	pútaojiǔ	(grape) wine
6. 杯	bēi	cup
7. 瓶	píng	bottle
8. 听	tīng	tin, can

练习 Exercises

一、替换练习。

Substitution drills.

A：喝点儿什么？
B：有茶吗？我喜欢喝茶。
A：有，你等等。
B：谢谢！

咖啡	啤酒
矿泉水	可口可乐

A：你想喝点儿什么？
B：随便。
A：那就喝杯咖啡吧。
B：好的。

杯	茶
点儿	饮料
点儿	酒
点儿	可乐

A：我想做生意。
B：那你得有钱。

去旅行	有时间
买汽车	先学开车
当总裁	学经济管理
进公司工作	了解公司

二、把下面的词组成句子。

Rearrange the following words into sentences.

1. 你　我　来　工作　酒吧　欢迎　的
2. 我　喝　饮料　想　点儿
3. 刚　三个月　汉语　我学
4. 他　努力　很　工作
5. 你们　在　随便　公司　走走　可以

三、完成对话。

Complete the following dialogues.

A：____________________？
B：我想喝杯咖啡。

A：你认识这个酒吧的老板吗？
B：________，他是________。

A：请问你是学什么的？
B：____________________。

A：你以后想做什么？
B：____________________。

四、模仿例句说话。

Complete the following sentences following the example.

例句：要学开车，得请师傅。

1. 想当老板，得________________。
2. 做生意，得________________。
3. 要会跑，先得________________。
4. 今天是太太生日，经理得________________。

五、用结构助词“得”完成句子。

Complete the following sentences with the structural particle 得.

1. 他送太太鲜花，太太高兴得________________。
2. 小谢刚学了三个月汉语，已经说得________________。
3. 这个公司你管理得________________。
4. 张师傅开车开得________________。
5. 今天是老师的生日，大家玩得________________。

六、会话练习。

Situational conversations.

情景1：请一个朋友去饭店或酒吧喝点儿什么。

Scene 1: Invite a friend to a restaurant or a bar to have a drink.

情景2：几个朋友或同事在一起，谈谈自己的工作，以前学什么，以后想做什么。

Scene 2: Several friends or colleagues gather together to talk about their work, what they learned before, and what they want to do in future.

七、给下面的拼音标上调号，然后朗读几遍。

Mark the tones of *pinyin* in the following passage and then read it aloud for several times.

Yi tian, Wang laoshi he tongxuemen qu yi ge jiuba. Jiuba de laoban shi ta de xuesheng Liu Liang. Liu Liang shi xue jingji de, gang gongzuo san nian jiu dang jingli le. Zhenni wen: “Zhe shi zhen de?” Liu Liang shuo: “Zhe shi zhen de.” Zhenni tingle hen gaoxing, shuo: “Wo ye xiang dang laoban, hai xiang dang zongcai ne!”

13

第十三课　你会说中国话吗（一）

Lesson 13　Can You Speak Chinese (I)

课　文

Text

在课上　Zài Kè Shang

王　老师：同学们，　你们 谁 会 说　中国话？
Wáng lǎoshī: Tóngxuémen, nǐmen shéi huì shuō Zhōngguóhuà?

杰克：　我 会 说，但是 说 得 不 好。
Jiékè: Wǒ huì shuō, dànshì shuō de bù hǎo.

珍妮：　我 才 开始 学习 汉语，只 会 说 一点儿。
Zhēnnī: Wǒ cái kāishǐ xuéxí Hànyǔ, zhǐ huì shuō yìdiǎnr.

王　老师：我 的 问题 不 是 这个 意思，我 知道 你们
Wáng lǎoshī: Wǒ de wèntí bú shì zhège yìsi, wǒ zhīdào nǐmen

都 会 说 一点儿 汉语 了。
dōu huì shuō yìdiǎnr Hànyǔ le.

珍妮：　那么，老师 的 意思 是 什么 呢？
Zhēnnī: Nàme, lǎoshī de yìsi shì shénme ne?

王　老师：我 先 考考 你们，怎么 请求 别人 帮助？
Wáng lǎoshī: Wǒ xiān kǎokao nǐmen, zěnme qǐngqiú biérén bāngzhù?

珍妮：　好 的，我 来 试试。
Zhēnnī: Hǎo de, wǒ lái shìshi.

珍妮：　喂，老头儿，北京 大学 在 哪儿？
Zhēnnī:　Wèi, lǎotóur, Běijīng Dàxué zài nǎr?

杰克：　喂，谁 姓“喂”？你 会不会 叫 人？
Jiékè:　Wèi, shéi xìng "wèi"? Nǐ huì bu huì jiào rén?

珍妮：　啊，对不起！老大爷，请问 北京 大学 在 哪儿？
Zhēnnī:　Ā, duìbuqǐ! Lǎodàye, qǐngwèn Běijīng Dàxué zài nǎr?

王 老师：这 就 对了，老大爷 一定 会 高高兴兴 地 告诉 你。
Wáng lǎoshī: Zhè jiù duì le, lǎodàye yídìng huì gāogāoxìngxìng de gàosu nǐ.

杰克：　请求 别人 帮助，应该 有 礼貌。
Jiékè:　Qǐngqiú biérén bāngzhù, yīnggāi yǒu lǐmào.

王 老师：好，再 来 一 次。
Wáng lǎoshī: Hǎo, zài lái yí cì.

山口：　开车 的，去 长城 饭店。
Shānkǒu:　Kāichē de, qù Chángchéng Fàndiàn.

杰克：　不 去！
Jiékè:　Bú qù!

山口：　喂，你 怎么 走 了？
Shānkǒu:　Wèi, nǐ zěnme zǒu le?

杰克：　他 当然 要 走 啦，谁 让 你 叫 他“开 车 的”？
Jiékè:　Tā dāngrán yào zǒu la, shéi ràng nǐ jiào tā "kāi chē de"?

山口：　我 应该 怎么 叫？
Shānkǒu:　Wǒ yīnggāi zěnme jiào?

杰克：　叫“师傅”呀！“师傅，去 长城 饭店。”
Jiékè:　Jiào "shīfu" ya! "Shīfu, qù Chángchéng Fàndiàn."

山口：　对，这样 有 礼貌，司机 还 会 不 高兴 吗？
Shānkǒu:　Duì, zhèyàng yǒu lǐmào, sījī hái huì bù gāoxìng ma?

王　老师：好，你们 明白 我的问题是 什么 意思 了 吗？
Wáng lǎoshī: Hǎo, nǐmen míngbai wǒ de wèntí shì shénme yìsi le ma?

珍妮：明白 了。
Zhēnnī: Míngbai le.

生词 New Words

1. 但是	dànshì	but, yet, nevertheless
2. 才	cái	only, not until
3. 开始	kāishǐ	to begin, to start
4. 只	zhǐ	only, merely
5. 一点儿	yìdiǎnr	a bit, a little
6. 考（试）	kǎo (shì)	to exam, to test
7. 请求	qǐngqiú	to ask, to request
8. 别人	biérén	other people, others
9. 帮助	bāngzhù	to help; assistance
10. 试	shì	to try, to test
11. 老头儿	lǎotóur	old man, old chap
12. 老大爷	lǎodàye	*a respectful form of address for men around one's father's age or older*
13. 一定	yídìng	certainly, surely; fixed, certain
14. 告诉	gàosu	to tell, to let…know
15. 应该	yīnggāi	should, ought to
16. 礼貌	lǐmào	courtesy, politeness, manners
17. 再	zài	again, once more
18. 次	cì	time, occurrence
19. 让	ràng	to let, to make
20. 这样	zhèyàng	such, this way, like this

专　名　Proper Nouns

1. 北京大学　Běijīng Dàxué　Peking University
2. 长城饭店　Chángchéng Fàndiàn　Great Wall Hotel

注　释
Notes

1　“会”，助动词，表示有（没有）某种能力。例如：

会, an auxiliary verb, indicates having (not having) a certain ability. For example:

1. 我会说汉语。
2. 她不会开车。
3. 王老师是个好老师，但不会做生意。

“会”，也表示可能。例如：

会 also expresses possibility. For example:

1. 你再等一会儿吧，他会来的。
2. 你这样说，他会生气的。
3. 他是一个好人，蒙人的事，他不会做。

2　“一点儿”，表示数量少而不确定，可做定语、宾语、主语。例如：

一点儿 means a small and uncertain number, and can be used as an attribute, an object or a subject. For example:

1. 他学了一点儿汉语。
2. 我买了一点儿蛋糕。
3. 杰克换了一点儿钱。

3　许多动词可以重叠使用，重叠后的动词，有尝试、经历时间短暂等附加意义。单音节动词的重叠形式是 AA，或 A 一 A；双音节动词的重叠形式是 ABAB。例如：

Many verbs can be duplicately used, which suggests a try or a short duration of time. Monosyllabic verbs, when duplicated, follow the pattern of AA or with 一 (one) inserted in between. The duplication of disyllabic verbs follows the pattern of ABAB. For example:

坐坐（坐一坐）	介绍介绍
等等（等一等）	学习学习
问问（问一问）	准备准备
说说（说一说）	欢迎欢迎

有些形容词也可以重叠，表示程度加深。重叠的形式是 AABB。例如：

Some adjectives can also be duplicated to indicate the deepening of the degree, and the pattern is AABB. For example:

高高兴兴	客客气气
明明白白	漂漂亮亮
安安全全	

4 "才"，副词，表示事情在不久前发生。例如：

才 is an adverb which means that something happened a short time ago. For example:

1. 他才走。
2. 我才下课。
3. 爸爸才回家。

补充生词 Additional New Words

1. 劳驾	láojià	to excuse me; may I trouble you; would you please
2. 大娘	dàniáng	aunt, wife of father's elder brother
3. 同志	tóngzhì	comrade
4. 路	lù	road, path, way
5. 声	shēng	sound, voice, tone
6. 句	jù	sentence

练习 Exercises

一、替换练习。

Substitution drills.

A：你会开车吗？

B：我不会，我的秘书会。

说英语	杰克
做生意	刘亮
写汉字	我的中国朋友
开酒瓶	酒吧服务员

A：我可以帮你做点儿什么吗？

B：请问在哪儿换钱？

怎么预订房间

怎么去国际邮局

你们经理在哪儿

在哪儿可以买到鲜花

二、把下面的词组成句子。

Rearrange the following words into sentences.

1. 我　汉语　说　会　一点儿
2. 我　明白　的　意思　你　不　一点儿　也
3. 你　问题　应该　有　告诉　我　什么
4. 明天　有　考试　我们
5. 我们　帮助　应该　大家　互相

三、完成对话。

Complete the following dialogues.

A：你会说汉语吗？

B：______________________。

A：叫司机“开车的”，司机会高兴吗？

B：__________，应该叫__________。

A：怎么问路才对？
B：________________________。

A：看见老人应该怎么称呼？
B：________________________。

A：你是什么时候开始学习汉语的？
B：________________________。

四、用“一点儿”完成下面的句子。

Complete the following sentences with 一点儿.

1. 他想　　　　挣钱
2. 妈妈　　　　买东西
3. 杰克　　　　吃饭
4. 安娜　　　　喝水

五、用动词或形容词重叠形式完成下列句子。

Complete the following sentences with the duplicate form of verbs or adjectives.

1. 我有问题，请你________我。（帮）
2. 后天我去旅行，要________。（准备）
3. 这句汉语你说得对不对，得________老师。（问）
4. 这句汉语你一定会说，请________吧。（试）
5. 老师要________你们，谁知道这句汉语怎么说才对？（考）
6. 秘书小姐对什么人都________的。（客气）
7. 今天是她的生日，我们得________的。（高兴）
8. 这个约会不应该________就取消。（随便）

六、用你学会的汉语谈谈怎么说、怎么做是没有礼貌的，怎么说、怎么做是有礼貌的。

Talk about what is polite and what is impolite in speaking and in acting.

七、会话练习。

Situational conversations.

情景 1：打电话给服务台预订房间。

Scene 1: Call the service desk to book a room.

情景 2：问路。

Scene 2: Ask the way.

八、阅读下面的一段话，然后用拼音把这段话写出来。

Read the following passage and then write it in *pinyin*.

说话，要会说。说的话不好听，别人听了会不高兴的。比如，问路、叫出租车、请求别人帮助，都要有礼貌。叫人的时候，应该叫一声“大爷”“大娘”“师傅”“同志”或者“先生”“小姐”；说一句“请问”“劳驾”。见人就叫“喂”“喂”的，这样没有礼貌，谁还会帮助你？

14

第十四课　你会说中国话吗（二）
Lesson 14　Can You Speak Chinese (Ⅱ)

课　文
Text

在课外　Zài Kè Wài

珍妮：	杰克，昨天 的 汉语 课 真 有 意思！
Zhēnnī:	Jiékè, zuótiān de Hànyǔ kè zhēn yǒu yìsi!
杰克：	是。想 说好 汉语，真 不 容易！
Jiékè:	Shì. Xiǎng shuōhǎo Hànyǔ, zhēn bù róngyì!
珍妮：	我们 一起 练习 练习 吧！
Zhēnnī:	Wǒmen yìqǐ liànxí liànxí ba!
杰克：	好 的。我 当 商店 售货员，你 当 顾客，怎么样？
Jiékè:	Hǎo de. Wǒ dāng shāngdiàn shòuhuòyuán, nǐ dāng gùkè, zěnmeyàng?
珍妮：	好，开始！
Zhēnnī:	Hǎo, kāishǐ!
杰克：	小姐，欢迎 您 来 购物！
Jiékè:	Xiǎojie, huānyíng nín lái gòuwù!
珍妮：	欢迎 购物？不 买，随便 看看，就 不行 吗？
Zhēnnī:	Huānyíng gòuwù? Bù mǎi, suíbiàn kànkan, jiù bùxíng ma?

杰克：　啊，欢迎！您 请 随便！
Jiékè: Ā, huānyíng! Nín qǐng suíbiàn!
珍妮：　看，你 说话 不得体，顾客 生气 了。
Zhēnnī: Kàn, nǐ shuōhuà bù détǐ, gùkè shēngqì le.

杰克：　好，我们 再试试。小姐，您 要 点儿 什么？
Jiékè: Hǎo, wǒmen zài shìshi. Xiǎojiě, nín yào diǎnr shénme?
珍妮：　什么 话？我 是 来 要 东西 的 吗？
Zhēnnī: Shénme huà? Wǒ shì lái yào dōngxi de ma?
杰克：　我 不是 那个 意思，请 不要 误会。
Jiékè: Wǒ bú shì nàge yìsi, qǐng búyào wùhuì.
珍妮：　是 我 误会了 你，还是 你 不会 说话？
Zhēnnī: Shì wǒ wùhuìle nǐ, háishì nǐ bú huì shuōhuà?
杰克：　啊，对不起！
Jiékè: Ā, duìbuqǐ!

杰克：　你 看，我 又 说错 了。
Jiékè: Nǐ kàn, wǒ yòu shuōcuò le.
珍妮：　你 不 能 说 “要 什么”。
Zhēnnī: Nǐ bù néng shuō “yào shénme”.
杰克：　我 应该 怎么 说？
Jiékè: Wǒ yīnggāi zěnme shuō?
珍妮：　应该 说：“小姐，您 想 买 点儿 什么？”
Zhēnnī: Yīnggāi shuō: “Xiǎojie, nín xiǎng mǎi diǎnr shénme?”
杰克：　不对！不对！我 不 买，看看 就 不行？
Jiékè: Búduì! Búduì! Wǒ bù mǎi, kànkan jiù bùxíng?
珍妮：　嗯，要是 这么 说，顾客 也 会 生气 的。
Zhēnnī: Ǹg, yàoshi zhème shuō, gùkè yě huì shēngqì de.
杰克：　那 该 怎么 说 呢？
Jiékè: Nà gāi zěnme shuō ne?
珍妮：　啊，太 难 了，我 也 不 会 了！
Zhēnnī: Ā, tài nán le, wǒ yě bú huì le!

生　词

New Words

1. 容易	róngyì	easy
2. 一起	yìqǐ	together
3. 练习	liànxí	to practice
4. 售货员	shòuhuòyuán	shop assistant, salesclerk
5. 顾客	gùkè	customer
6. 购物	gòuwù	to purchase, to buy, to go shopping
7. 看	kàn	to look (round)
8. 得体	détǐ	appropriate, to be fitting one's position or suited to the occasion
9. 东西	dōngxi	thing
10. 误会	wùhuì	to misunderstand, to mistake
11. 又	yòu	again, also
12. 能	néng	may, can, to be able to
13. 嗯	ǹg	*an interjection used to show different tones*
14. 要是	yàoshi	if, in case; to suppose
15. 该	gāi	should
16. 难	nán	difficult, hard, troublesome

注　释

Notes

1　“又”和“再”，两个都是副词，都可以表示同一个动作、行为的重复，但用法不同。对于已实现的行为或动作，只能用“又”；而对未实现、或将要实现、或假想的动作、行为，则要用“再”。请认真比较下面的句子：

又 and 再 are both adverbs to express repetition of the same motion or action, but they are used differently. For a motion or action that has been fulfilled, only 又 can be used. For a motion or action that has not been fulfilled, or one that will be fulfilled in the future, or a fictitious one, 再 should be used. Please compare the following sentences carefully:

1. 他前天来了，昨天又来了。
   请你明天再来。

2. 时候还早，再坐会儿吧！
   他真的又坐下了。

3. 你已经喝了很多啤酒，可不能再喝了。
   他喝了很多啤酒，又吃了很多蛋糕。

2 “要是”，连词，表示假设，多用于口语。例如：

要是 is a conjunction expressing a supposition. It is used more often in spoken Chinese. For example:

1. 他要是不喜欢，你就别给他买。
2. 你要是能来，那就太好了。
3. 你要是不喜欢听，我就不说了。

3 “能”，助动词，表示有能力做某事，或条件、环境、情理允许做某事。例如：

能 is an auxiliary verb, indicating the ability to do something, or that the conditions, circumstances, or accepted code of human conduct permit somebody to do something. For example:

1. 我能帮助你。
2. 这种苹果能卖5元钱一斤。
3. 他家里今天有事，不能来上班。
4. 经理不能没有秘书。

注意：“能”和“会”都是助动词，学生常常误用，要注意辨别这两个词的异同。“会”和“能”，都可表示有能力做某事，这种情况下，两个词可以互换。例如：

Please note that both 能 and 会 are auxiliary verbs, and students often misuse them. Special attention should be paid to the similarities and differences between these two words. Both 会 and 能 can be used to express the ability to do something. Under such circumstances, these two words can be used interchangeably. For example:

1. 小孩儿一岁半了，会走路了。
2. 小孩儿一岁半了，能走路了。

下面例子中的“能”，表示条件、环境允许，或丧失的能力又恢复了，不能换用“会”。

能 in the following examples expresses permission by the conditions, or circumstances, or the recovery of a lost ability, and it cannot be replaced by 会.

1. 这儿能游泳吗？
   这儿不能游泳。

2. 我能（在办公室）抽烟吗？
   你不能（在办公室）抽烟。

3. 学了一个月，他会开车了。
   他的手恢复了，（又）能开车了。（以前骨折了，不能开车；现在恢复了，又能开车了。）

表示达到某种程度、水平、效率等，只能用“能”，不能用“会”。例如：

To express reaching a certain extent, level or efficiency, only 能 can be used, and it cannot be replaced by 会. For example:

1. 他能认 800 个汉语生词了。
2. 他的英语很好，能当大学英语老师。
3. 他三分钟能喝六瓶啤酒。

补充生词 Additional New Words

1. 有事儿	yǒu shìr	to be occupied
2. 为	wèi	for, because of, for the sake of
3. 效劳	xiàoláo	to work for, to work in the service of

练习
Exercises

一、替换练习。
Substitution drills.

A：我们一起去商店好吗？
B：对不起，我要去邮局。

教室	宿舍
喝咖啡	上班
学习汉语	找工作
问老师	打电话

A：你能帮我叫辆出租车吗？
B：对不起，我有事儿，你自己叫吧！

练习一下口语
预订一个房间
找一下饭店经理
送一枝鲜花给安娜

二、把下面的词组成句子。
Rearrange the following words into sentences.

1. 你　真　说　话　有意思　的
2. 汉语　难　吗　很　学习
3. 星期天　我们　商店　购物　去
4. 我　买　东西　去　商店　点儿
5. 我　你　意思　误会　了　对不起　的

三、完成对话。
Complete the following dialogues.

A：你什么时候去商店买东西？
B：________________。

A：商店的售货员都很有礼貌吗？
B：________________。

A：______________________？
B：我随便看看。

A：我能学好汉语吗？
B：当然，______________。

四、选择“又”或“再”填入下列各句。

Fill in the blanks with 又 or 再.

1. 他______开始学习汉语了。
2. 老板想自己先去中国旅行，以后______让太太去。
3. 我刚换了100美元，______换50美元。
4. 秘书为老板预订了房间，______预订了车。
5. 司机已经开了5个小时车了，不能______开车了。
6. 他喝了______喝，已经不能______喝了。
7. 他还想______买一点儿蛋糕。
8. 他已经听明白了，你就不要______说了。

五、在下列句子中填写“会”或“能”，如能互换，讲讲有什么不同。

Fill in the blanks with 会 or 能. If they are interchangeable, tell their differences if any.

1. 学了三个月汉语，应该______说一点儿汉语了。
2. 买小贩的东西______砍价吗？
3. 你______用汉语打电话吗？
4. 蒙人的事，我们不______做。
5. 她______自己开车上班了。
6. 经理是个好人，______帮助朋友的事，他一定______帮助。
7. 现在银行不开门，不______换钱。
8. 不______走，怎么______跑？

六、模仿例句说话。

Make sentences following the example.

例句：要是没有他的帮助，我就不能来中国。

1. 要是　钱　旅行
2. 要是　效劳　高兴
3. 要是　喜欢　买
4. 要是　告诉　生气
5. 要是　想学好汉语　练习

七、会话练习。

Situational conversation.

情景：几个顾客在商店购物，一个顾客说话很得体，一个顾客很没礼貌，一个顾客会说一点儿汉语，听不明白，也说不明白。

售货员小姐怎么为他们效劳？

Scene: Several customers are shopping. One customer speaks in appropriate terms and the other is rude. Another one can speak a little Chinese, but he can neither understand what is said to him nor make himself understood.

How would the salesgirl serve them?

八、给下面的拼音标上调号，然后朗读几遍。

Mark the tones of *pinyin* in the following passage and then read it aloud for several times.

Yi tian, Zhenni he Jieke zai ke wai lianxi shuo Hanyu. Jieke dang shangdian fuwuyuan, Zhenni dang guke. Zhenni qu mai dongxi. Keshi, zhege fuwuyuan haoxiang bu tai hui shuohua, zenme shuo, guke dou shengqi, zheyang zenme neng zuohao shengyi ne? Ō, Jieke he Zhenni, hai yinggai haohaor lianxi shuo Hanyu.

15

第十五课 你会买东西吗（一）

Lesson 15 Do You Know How to Make Purchases (Ⅰ)

课 文

Text

在课上 Zài Kè Shang

王 老师：同学们，你们 会 买 东西 吗？
Wáng lǎoshī：Tóngxuémen, nǐmen huì mǎi dōngxi ma?
珍妮：会。一 手 交 钱，一 手 交 货。
Zhēnnī：Huì. Yì shǒu jiāo qián, yì shǒu jiāo huò.
杰克：这么 简单？
Jiékè：Zhème jiǎndān?
王 老师：你们 试试，看看 是不是 这么 简单。
Wáng lǎoshī：Nǐmen shìshi, kànkan shì bú shì zhème jiǎndān.

杰克：你 好，苹果 多少 钱 一 斤？
Jiékè：Nǐ hǎo, píngguǒ duōshao qián yì jīn?
珍妮：杰克，不 能 在 这儿 买。
Zhēnnī：Jiékè, bù néng zài zhèr mǎi.
杰克：怎么？你 不 会 砍价？
Jiékè：Zěnme? Nǐ bú huì kǎnjià?
珍妮：不 是 不 会 砍价，是 不 能 在 这儿 砍价！
Zhēnnī：Bú shì bú huì kǎnjià, shì bù néng zài zhèr kǎnjià!
杰克：为 什么？
Jiékè：Wèi shénme?

珍妮：这个 卖 苹果 的，是 我 朋友 的爸爸！
Zhēnnī: Zhège mài píngguǒ de, shì wǒ péngyou de bàba!

Jiékè: Hǎo ba.
杰克：好吧。

珍妮：苹果 多少 钱 一 斤？
Zhēnnī: Píngguǒ duōshao qián yì jīn?

小贩：十二 块 三 斤。
Xiǎofàn: Shí'ér kuài sān jīn.

珍妮：十 块 三 斤，卖 不 卖？
Zhēnnī: Shí kuài sān jīn, mài bú mài?

小贩：十 块 两 斤 半！
Xiǎofàn: Shí kuài liǎng jīn bàn!

珍妮：什么？ 还是 四 块 钱 一 斤？
Zhēnnī: Shénme? Hái shì sì kuài qián yì jīn?

杰克：老板，你 真 会 蒙 人！
Jiékè: Lǎobǎn, nǐ zhēn huì mēng rén!

珍妮：十 块 钱 三 斤 不 卖，我们 走 了！
Zhēnnī: Shí kuài qián sān jīn bú mài, wǒmen zǒu le!

小贩：好，好，十 块 三 斤！
Xiǎofàn: Hǎo, hǎo, shí kuài sān jīn!

珍妮：怎么样？ 我 砍掉 他 两 块 钱！
Zhēnnī: Zěnmeyàng? Wǒ kǎndiào tā liǎng kuài qián!

杰克：你 真 会 买 东西！
Jiékè: Nǐ zhēn huì mǎi dōngxi!

生 词
New Words

1. 手 shǒu hand
2. 货 huò goods, commodity

3. 简单	jiǎndān	simple
4. 苹果	píngguǒ	apple
5. 斤	jīn	half a kilo, *jin*
6. 砍	kǎn	to cut, to chop
7. 价（格）	jià (gé)	price
8. 卖	mài	to sell
9. 小贩	xiǎofàn	peddler
10. 两	liǎng	two
11. 蒙人	mēng rén	to deceive sb.
12. 怎么样	zěnmeyàng	how about, what's it like
13. 掉	diào	to fall, to drop, to remove

注 释 Notes

1 “二”和“两”，都是数字“2”，但“二”可以单独使用，“两”则不能。例如数数，要说“一、二、三”，不能说“一、两、三”。但在量词前边，一般要用“两”。例如：

Both 二 and 两 indicate the numeral 2, but 二 can be used independently while 两 can't. For instance, when counting, we should say 一, 二, 二, but and not 一, 两, 三. But when 二 is used before a measure word, it is generally pronounced as 两. For example:

两个学生
两个小时
两元钱

2 “怎么”和“怎么样”，都是疑问代词，用来询问性质、状况、方式等，“怎么”常用做状语。“怎么样”常用做谓语，也可做状语。“怎么”做状语时，还可用来询问原因，但“怎么样”则没有这种用法。

Both 怎么 and 怎么样 are interrogative pronouns. They are used to ask about the nature, condition, or way. 怎么 is often used as an adverbial. 怎么样 is often used as a predicate, or sometimes as an adverbial. When 怎么 is used as an adverbial, it can also be used for asking about the reason, but 怎么样 cannot be used this way.

“怎么样”，可以用来征求他人的意见和对他人或事物的评价，“怎么”则不能。

怎么样 can be used to ask for opinions or comments on other people or things, while 怎么 cannot be used this way.

1. 他怎么还不来？
2. 我们怎么去长城？
3. 你的汉语学得怎么样了？
4. 这个服务员怎么样？好不好？

补充生词 Additional New Words

1. 葡萄	pútao	grape
2. 香蕉	xiāngjiāo	banana
3. 西瓜	xīguā	watermelon
4. 橘子	júzi	tangerine
5. 岁	suì	year
6. 抽烟	chōu yān	to smoke

练　习 Exercises

一、替换练习。

Substitution drills.

A：你会开车吗？
B：我会开车，但是我现在不能开车。我没有车了。

买车	不会开车
做生意	没有钱
写汉字	没有笔
抽烟	正在上班

香蕉	三斤	三斤三两
葡萄	四斤	四斤六两
橘子	五斤	五斤一两

A：老板，买水果。
B：买什么水果？
A：苹果。
B：您买几斤？
A：两斤。
B：这是两斤半，行吗？
A：行。

二、把下面的词组成句子。

Rearrange the following words into sentences.

1. 这　简单　很　事
2. 多少　一斤　香蕉　钱
3. 哪儿　买　水果　可以　到
4. 你　不　问　买　价　东西　吗
5. 生意　怎么样　的　你　做　得

三、完成对话。

Complete the following dialogues.

A：你买小贩的东西吗？
B：______________________。

A：你买东西的时候，喜欢砍价吗？
B：______________________。

A：现在苹果多少钱一斤？
B：______________________。

A：______________________？
B：这儿的水果很不错。

A：你喜欢去哪儿买东西？
B：______________________。

四、在下列句子中填写"怎么"或"怎么样"。

Fill in the blanks with 怎么 or 怎么样.

1. 经理________请求，太太都不让他抽烟。
2. 你汉语学得不错，你是________学习的？
3. 你的生意现在做得________了？
4. 顾客________说，服务员也不生气。
5. ________才能不堵车呢？

五、模仿例句说话。

Make sentences following the example.

例句：不是不会砍价，是不能在这儿砍价。

1. 他的	我的
2. 学生	经理
3. 看书	看电视
4. 星期一	星期三

六、会话练习。

Situational conversation.

情景：两个顾客，一个小贩。

Scene: Here are two customers and a vendor.

七、读拼音，写汉字。

Read the following passage in *pinyin* and then write it out in Chinese characters.

Jiékè hé Zhēnnī qù mǎi píngguǒ. Zhēnnī shuō tā huì kǎn jià. Jiékè xiǎng shìshi Zhēnnī shì bú shì zhēn de huì kǎnjià, jiù hé tā yìqǐ qù mǎi píngguǒ. Zhēnnī kǎnle bàntiān jià, gāogāoxìngxìng mǎile sān jīn píngguǒ.

16

第十六课　你会买东西吗（二）

Lesson 16　Do You Know How to Make Purchases（II）

课　文

Text

在课外　Zài Kè Wài

珍妮：　杰克，你 喜欢 看　广告　吗？
Zhēnnī:　Jiékè,　nǐ xǐhuan kàn guǎnggào ma?

杰克：　不 喜欢 也 要 看 啊！
Jiékè:　Bù xǐhuan yě yào kàn a!

珍妮：　为　什么？
Zhēnnī:　Wèi shénme?

杰克：　不 看，怎么 买　东西？
Jiékè:　Bú kàn, zěnme mǎi dōngxi?

珍妮：　看 了，就 会 买 吗？
Zhēnnī:　Kàn le,　jiù huì mǎi ma?

杰克：　那 当然，不 信，我们 就 试试。
Jiékè:　Nà dāngrán, bú xìn, wǒmen jiù shìshi.

珍妮：　那……　我们 去 买 一 个 西瓜 吧！
Zhēnnī:　Nà…　Wǒmen qù mǎi yí gè xīguā ba!

杰克：　好。
Jiékè:　Hǎo.

珍妮：　杰克，你 看 这 小 黑板　上　写 的 字！
Zhēnnī:　Jiékè,　nǐ kàn zhè xiǎo hēibǎn shang xiě de zì!

杰克： 一斤一元五角，正宗美国西瓜118。
Jiékè: Yì jīn yì yuán wǔ jiǎo, zhèngzōng Měiguó xīguā 118.
缺点：太甜。
Quēdiǎn: tài tián.
珍妮： 中国卖的美国西瓜，你吃过吗？
Zhēnnī: Zhōngguó mài de Měiguó xīguā, nǐ chīguo ma?
杰克： 还没吃过。
Jiékè: Hái méi chīguo.
珍妮： 怎么样，买吗？
Zhēnnī: Zěnmeyàng, mǎi ma?
杰克： 买！这瓜甜，我爱吃。
Jiékè: Mǎi! Zhè guā tián, wǒ ài chī.

杰克： 西瓜多少钱一斤？
Jiékè: Xīguā duōshao qián yì jīn?
小贩： 一块五！
Xiǎofàn: Yí kuài wǔ!
杰克： 太贵了！能便宜一点儿吗？
Jiékè: Tài guì le! Néng piányi yìdiǎnr ma?
小贩： 不能。这是正宗美国118。
Xiǎofàn: Bù néng. Zhè shì zhèngzōng Měiguó 118.
杰克： 你这小黑板上写的不蒙人吧？
Jiékè: Nǐ zhè xiǎo hēibǎn shang xiě de bù mēng rén ba?
小贩： 哪能啊？
Xiǎofàn: Nǎ néng a?
杰克： 好，老板，挑一个！
Jiékè: Hǎo, lǎobǎn, tiāo yí gè!
小贩： 好咧！
Xiǎofàn: Hǎo lie!
杰克： 多少钱？
Jiékè: Duōshao qián?
小贩： 十一斤半，一共十七块两毛五，给十七
Xiǎofàn: Shíyī jīn bàn, yígòng shíqī kuài liǎng máo wǔ, gěi shíqī

块 钱 吧。
kuài qián ba.

杰克：开 一 个 口子。
Jiékè: Kāi yí gè kǒuzi.

小贩：好 咧！
Xiǎofàn: Hǎo lie!

杰克：老板，这 瓜 怎么 一点儿 也 不 甜 啊？
Jiékè: Lǎobǎn, zhè guā zěnme yìdiǎnr yě bù tián a?

小贩：这儿 写着 呢，缺点 是 太 甜，优点 就 是 不 甜 啰！
Xiǎofàn: Zhèr xiězhe ne, quēdiǎn shì tài tián, yōudiǎn jiù shì bù tián luo!

杰克：啊？你 这 广告……
Jiékè: Á? Nǐ zhè guǎnggào…

生词 New Words

1. 广告 guǎnggào advertisement
2. （相）信 (xiāng) xìn to believe
3. 黑板 hēibǎn blackboard
4. 写 xiě to write
5. 字 zì word, character
6. 正宗 zhèngzōng authentic, genuine
7. 缺点 quēdiǎn shortcoming
8. 甜 tián sweet
9. 吃 chī to eat
10. 过 guo *a particle indicating a past action or a state*
11. 贵 guì expensive
12. 便宜 piányi cheap
13. 挑（选） tiāo (xuǎn) to choose, to select, to pick out

14. 咧	lie	*a dialectal particle*
15. 一共	yígòng	altogether, in all
16. 口子	kǒuzi	opening, hole, cut
17. 着	zhe	*a particle indicating that an action is in progress or a state is continuing*
18. 优点	yōudiǎn	merit, strong point
19. 啰	luo	*a particle*

注 释
Notes

“着”“了”“过”，动态助词。汉语里的动词，词形本身没有时态变化。动词的时态，是通过助词“着”“了”“过”来表示的。

着, 了 and 过 are tense particles. Verbs in Chinese do not have inflections in form to indicate the change of tenses. Tenses of verbs are expressed through such particles as 着, 了, and 过.

1 “着”，表示动作正在进行或状态正在持续，有时跟副词“正”“在”“正在”配合使用。例如：

着 indicates that an action is in progress or a state is continuing. It is often used together with such adverbs as 正, 在 or 正在. For example:

1. 他开着车还打电话。
2. 她吃着东西还说个不停。
3. 我们正吃着饭，客人来了。
4. 我们说着说着，她就生气了。

2 “了”，表示动作已经完成，可用于实际已经发生的事情的完成，也可用于想象中将要发生的事情或假设可能发生的事情的完成。例如：

了 indicates that an action is completed, which can either be the completion of an action that has actually occurred, or the completion of an action that one thinks will happen or an action that one presumes may happen. For example:

1. 小王来了，小谢没有来。
2. 等经理来了，我告诉他。
3. 你学会砍价了吗？
4. 我当了大老板，也要感谢你。

3 “过”表示过去曾经有这样的事情或有这样的经验。例如：

过 refers to things in the past or past experience. For example:

1. 你去过上海吗？
2. 我去过上海。
3. 他还没有去过上海。
4. 去过上海，就知道上海多么漂亮了。

补充生词 Additional New Word

欺骗	qīpiàn	to deceive, to cheat

练习 Exercises

一、替换练习。

Substitution drills.

A：这种西瓜怎么样？
B：我不买。
A：为什么？
B：太甜，我不喜欢。

手机	贵	我没钱
苹果	小	不好吃
茶	便宜	不好喝

A：你的优点是什么？
B：喜欢学习。
A：你的缺点是什么？
B：学了就忘。

看书	不爱上班
交朋友	总让朋友不高兴
说话	说话不得体
帮助人	太爱钱

二、把下面的词组成句子。

Rearrange the following words into sentences.

1. 你　她　相信　应该
2. 广告　事　告诉　多　你　很　可以
3. 便宜　好货　有　也
4. 你　挑　吗　会　西瓜
5. 钱　一共　三斤　多少　苹果

三、完成对话。

Complete the following dialogues.

A：你相信广告吗？
B：________________。

A：你为什么喜欢买便宜货？
B：________________。

A：________________？
B：三斤苹果，一斤香蕉，一共是13.50元。

A：________________？
B：不能再便宜了。

四、在下列各句中填写“着”“了”“过”，如果“了”“过”都可填，讲讲二者的不同。

Fill in the blanks with 着, 了 or 过. If both 了 and 过 can be used, tell their differences if any.

1. 她正挑______，售货员走来了，说：“我可以帮你吗？”
2. 我给你打______电话，你不在。
3. 你们已经收______我的停车费，怎么还要收？
4. 我学______半年汉语，可是都忘了。
5. 他用自己的钱帮助______很多朋友。
6. 你去______长城吗？
7. 老板喜欢看______价格谈生意。
8. 你在中国坐______出租车吗？
9. 他们正说______什么，我去了，他们就都不说话了。
10. 他用旅行支票兑换______现金。

五、模仿例句说话。

Make sentences following the example.

例句：我们去买一个便宜点儿的西瓜吧！

1. 买	葡萄酒
2. 买	苹果
3. 喝	橙汁
4. 去	酒吧
5. 听	课

例句：你看这小黑板上写的字！

1. 服务台	留的
2. 广告	介绍的
3. 矿泉水瓶	写的
4. 约会时	说的
5. 发票上	写的

例句：这瓜怎么一点儿也不甜啊！

1. 东西	便宜
2. 这儿	好玩
3. 苹果	好吃
4. 黑板上写的字	明白

六、用你学过的词语写一则推销水果的广告。

Use the learned words to write an ad for promoting the sale of fruits.

七、会话练习。

Situational conversations.

情景 1：买水果，你要挑，老板不让你挑。

Scene 1: You are buying fruits. You want to pick and choose, and the vender doesn't allow you to.

情景 2：买水果，老板让你挑，你不会挑。

Scene 2: You are buying fruits. You are allowed to pick and choose, but you don't know how to.

八、读拼音，写汉字。

Read the following passage in *pinyin*, and then write it out in Chinese characters.

Mài xīguā de xiǎofàn zài xiǎo hēibǎn shang xiězhe: zhèngzōng Měiguó xīguā 118. Quēdiǎn: tài tiàn. Zhè shì shénme yìsi ne? Shì shuō tā mài de xīguā tài tián, zhè shì yí gè quēdiǎn, háishi shuō xīguā tài tián, shì yí gè quēdiǎn, tā de xīguā méiyǒu zhège quēdiǎn, yì diǎnr yě bù tián? Jiékè shì zěnme lǐjiě de ne? Tā lǐjiě de duì ma?

17

第十七课　我们离不开它（一）

Lesson 17　We Can't Do Without It (Ⅰ)

课　文

Text

在课上　Zài Kè Shang

王　老师：同学们，　我 问 你们 一 个 问题，你们 每
Wáng lǎoshī: Tóngxuémen, wǒ wèn nǐmen yí gè wèntí, nǐmen měi
天 离 不 开 的 是……
tiān lí bu kāi de shì…

杰克：珍妮 以前 每 天 都 离 不 开 她 的 妈妈。
Jiékè: Zhēnnī yǐqián měi tiān dōu lí bu kāi tā de māma.

山口：珍妮 还 离 不 开 她 的 芭比 娃娃。
Shānkǒu: Zhēnnī hái lí bu kāi tā de Bābǐ wáwa.

王　老师：我 问 你们 现在 每 天 离 不 开 的 是 什么？
Wáng lǎoshī: Wǒ wèn nǐmen xiànzài měi tiān lí bu kāi de shì shénme?

珍妮：老 师，是 手机，我们 一 分钟 都 离 不
Zhēnnī: Lǎo shī, shì shǒujī, wǒmen yì fēnzhōng dōu lí bu
开 它！
kāi tā!

杰克：对！ 我们 都 离 不 开 它。
Jiékè: Duì! wǒmen dōu lí bu kāi tā.

王　老师：不 知道 从 哪 一 天 开始，人们 突然 发现，
Wáng lǎoshī: Bù zhīdào cóng nǎ yì tiān kāishǐ, rénmen tūrán fāxiàn,

不管 是 年轻人 还是 老人，每 个 人 手 里，
bùguǎn shì niánqīngrén háishi lǎorén，měi gè rén shǒu li，
都 拿着 一 个 手机。
dōu názhe yí gè shǒujī.

山口：老师，这 是 好 事，说明 手机 普及 了。
Shānkǒu：Lǎoshī，zhè shì hǎo shì，shuōmíng shǒujī pǔjí le.

王 老师：你们 说 得 很 对。那么，你们 还 有 什么 发现 吗？
Wáng lǎoshī：Nǐmen shuō de hěn duì. Nàme，nǐmen hái yǒu shénme fāxiàn ma?

杰克：我 发现，很 多 人 总是 低 头 玩儿 手机，
Jiékè：Wǒ fāxiàn，hěn duō rén zǒngshì dī tóu wánr shǒujī，
不管 是 上课、走路 还是 坐 车，都 这样。
bùguǎn shì shàngkè、zǒulù háishi zuò chē，dōu zhèyàng.

山口：我 听说，有 个 大学生 坐 公交车，因为
Shānkǒu：Wǒ tīngshuō，yǒu gè dàxuéshēng zuò gōngjiāochē，yīnwèi
玩儿 手机 坐 过 站 了，就 一下 拉开 窗户，
wánr shǒujī zuò guò zhàn le，jiù yíxià lākāi chuānghu，
从 窗户 跳下 车 了。
cóng chuānghu tiàoxià chē le.

珍妮：这 多 危险 啊！
Zhēnnī：Zhè duō wēixiǎn a!

王 老师：是 啊。下 课 后，大家 一起 好好儿 聊聊，
Wáng lǎoshī：Shì a. Xià kè hòu，dàjiā yìqǐ hǎohāor liáoliao，
怎样 安全、有效 地 使用 手机，好 不 好？
zěnyàng ānquán、yǒuxiào de shǐyòng shǒujī，hǎo bù hǎo?

生 词
New Words

1. 离开 líkāi to leave
2. 芭比娃娃 Bābǐ wáwa Barbie

3. 从	cóng	from
4. 突然	tūrán	suddenly
5. 发现	fāxiàn	to find
6. 不管	bùguǎn	regardless of
7. 年轻人	niánqīngrén	young people
8. 老人	lǎorén	senior people, the elderly
9. 说明	shuōmíng	to show
10. 普及	pǔjí	popular
11. 低头	dītóu	to lower one's head
12. 上课	shàngkè	to attend class, to give a lecture
13. 听说	tīngshuō	it is said that
14. 公交车	gōngjiāochē	bus
15. 站	zhàn	stop, station
16. 拉开	lākāi	to open
17. 窗户	chuānghu	window
18. 跳	tiào	to jump
19. 多	duō	how
20. 危险	wēixiǎn	dangerous
21. 聊	liáo	to chat
22. 安全	ānquán	safe
23. 有效	yǒuxiào	effective
24. 使用	shǐyòng	to use

注　释

Notes

1　“离开”，动词，可以独立运用，也可以在中间嵌入“不”或“得”，构成“离不开”或“离得开”的格式。例如：

The verb 离开 can be used independently or in the forms 离不开 and 离得开. For example:

1. 听说，他离开美国后，去了英国。
2. 孩子的成长离不开父母的关心和照顾。
3. 珍妮离不开她的芭比娃娃。

2 “不管……都……”，这是口语中常用到的一个句式。表示在任何条件下结果或结论都不会改变。例如：

不管……都…… is a sentence structure often used in spoken Chinese. It means that the result or conclusion will not change under any condition. For example:

1. 不管你听说了什么，都要告诉我。
2. 不管是上课、走路还是坐车，他都在玩手机。
3. 不管是手机，还是电脑，我们现在都离不开。
4. 不管你去不去，我都要去。

3 “听说”，是“听……说”缩略成的一个联合结构动词。“听”后可以明确说出消息来源，也可以省略消息来源，缩略成“听说”的形式。例如：

听说 (to hear of), abbreviated from 听……说, is a verb of joint structure. 听 can be followed by the clear source of news or be abbreviated as 听说 without the source. For example:

1. 我听杰克说，他的手机不见了。
2. 我听很多人说，他一分钟都离不开手机。
3. 我听说杰克不抽烟。
4. 我听说珍妮的妈妈要来中国了。

补充生词 Additional New Words

1. 电	diàn	electricity
2. 电脑	diànnǎo	computer
3. 接通	jiētōng	to connect

练习 Exercises

一、替换练习。

Substitution drills.

A：你离开爸爸妈妈多久了？

B：两个月了。

A：你想他们吗？

B：不想。

家乡	一年	家乡	有点儿想
女朋友	一个月	她	想极了
学校	三年	学校的同学	不想
中国	五年	中国的饭菜	很想

A：我听说杰克买新手机了。

B：你听谁说的？

C：听安娜说的，你听说了吗？

D：我没有听说。

有	女朋友	山口
离开	学校	珍妮
去	酒吧	他同学
回	美国	老师

二、把下面的词组成句子。

Rearrange the following words into sentences.

1. 手机　每天　我　离不开　都
2. 手机　马路　玩儿　过　危险　很
3. 手　手机　着　每　拿　人　都　个　里
4. 是　有效　什么　手机　使用　说　你　地

三、完成对话。

Complete the following dialogues.

A：你想换新手机吗？
B：______________________。
A：为什么？
B：______________________。

A：______________________？
B：我每天都要给妈妈打电话。
A：______________________？
B：告诉爸爸妈妈我每天的生活、学习。

A：你离得开手机吗？
B：______________________。
A：为什么？
B：______________________。
A：对，有手机太方便了。

四、选择合适的词，填在下面句子中的适当地方。

Choose the proper word and put it in the right place in each of the following sentences.

不管　还是　都

1. 是你来，他来，我高兴。
2. 你听不听我的话，我是为你好。
3. 坐公交，骑自行车，可以去天安门。
4. 别人怎么说，他没听见，该做什么还做什么。
5. 刮风下雨，他去学校上课。
6. 不管你欢迎不欢迎，我要去看你。

五、模仿例句说话。

Complete the following sentences following the example.

例句：每个人都拿着手机，说明手机普及了。

1. 他考得很好	努力
2. 房间里没灯了	没有人
3. 每人都有电脑	生活现代化
4. 到处都是汽车	汽车普及

例句：我突然发现坐过站了。

1. 手机没有电
2. 回国
3. 有女朋友
4. 普及

六、会话练习。

Situational conversations.

情景 1：和朋友说说你走在大街上或公园里，看到的一种普通现象。

Scene 1: Talk to a friend about a common phenomenon you see on the street or in the park.

情景 2：和朋友说说你在北京生活期间，发现的北京的变化。

Scene 2: Talk to a friend about the changes in Beijing that you found during your stay in Beijing.

七、朗读下面的一段话，然后用拼音把这段话写出来。

Read the following passage, and then write it in *pinyin*.

昨天，安娜想告诉我一些好玩儿的事。可是，她打我的手机，怎么也打不通。"什么时候？""昨天下午。""啊，我的手机没有电了！""我以为你不要我这个朋友了呢！""那哪儿能啊。对不起！"

18

第十八课 我们离不开它（二）

Lesson 18 We Can't Do Without It(Ⅱ)

课 文 Text

在课外 Zài Kè Wài

珍妮： 杰克！山口！ 我们 一起 来 完成 作业 吧。
Zhēnnī: Jiékè! Shānkǒu! Wǒmen yìqǐ lái wánchéng zuòyè ba.

山口： 我 先 问 你们 两 个，你们 离 得 开 手机 吗？
Shānkǒu: Wǒ xiān wèn nǐmen liǎng gè, nǐmen lí de kāi shǒujī ma?

杰克： 当然 离 不 开！我 每 天 都 要 和 女朋友 约会，没有 手机 怎么 行？
Jiékè: Dāngrán lí bu kāi! Wǒ měi tiān dōu yào hé nǚpéngyou yuēhuì, méiyǒu shǒujī zěnme xíng?

珍妮： 我 每 天 要 给 妈妈 打 电话，当然 也 离 不 开 它！
Zhēnnī: Wǒ měi tiān yào gěi māma dǎ diànhuà, dāngrán yě lí bu kāi tā!

杰克： 对，现在 用 手机 上网 很 方便，所以 大家 都 离 不 开 手机 了。
Jiékè: Duì, xiànzài yòng shǒujī shàngwǎng hěn fāngbiàn, suǒyǐ dàjiā dōu lí bu kāi shǒujī le.

山口： 对！我 喜欢 用 手机 叫 外卖！
Shānkǒu: Duì! Wǒ xǐhuan yòng shǒujī jiào wàimài!

珍妮： 我 知道，你 很 爱 睡 懒觉， 常常 不 去
Zhēnnī: Wǒ zhīdào, nǐ hěn ài shuì lǎnjiào, chángcháng bú qù
食堂 吃 饭，就 叫 外卖。
shítáng chī fàn, jiù jiào wàimài.

山口： 是 啊！ 那 多 方便！
Shānkǒu: Shì a! Nà duō fāngbiàn!

杰克： 我 想 吃 汉堡，也 叫 外卖。
Jiékè: Wǒ xiǎng chī hànbǎo, yě jiào wàimài.

珍妮： 其实，不 只是 叫 外卖，现在 几乎 没有 用
Zhēnnī: Qíshí, bù zhǐshì jiào wàimài, xiànzài jīhū méiyǒu yòng
手机 办 不 了 的 事。
shǒujī bàn bu liǎo de shì.

山口： 对！我 就 很 久 没 去 银行、 商店 了，现在
Shānkǒu: Duì! Wǒ jiù hěn jiǔ méi qù yínháng, shāngdiàn le, xiànzài
都 用 手机 在 网 上 买 东西 了。
dōu yòng shǒujī zài wǎng shang mǎi dōngxi le.

杰克： 打 的、预订 机票、给 女朋友 买 礼物，都
Jiékè: Dǎ dī, yùdìng jīpiào, gěi nǚpéngyou mǎi lǐwù, dōu
能 用 手机。
néng yòng shǒujī.

珍妮： 我们 变 得 越 来 越 懒 了。
Zhēnnī: Wǒmen biàn de yuè lái yuè lǎn le.

杰克： 不 对！ 我 们 是 变 得 越 来 越 会 享受
Jiékè: Bú duì! Wǒ men shì biàn de yuè lái yuè huì xiǎngshòu
生活 了。
shēnghuó le.

山口： 享受 现代化 的 生活！
Shānkǒu: Xiǎngshòu xiàndàihuà de shēnghuó!

杰克： 现在 还 有 微信，能 交到 很 多 朋友，
Jiékè: Xiànzài hái yǒu wēixìn, néng jiāodào hěn duō péngyou,
还 能 随时 了解 新闻。
hái néng suíshí liǎojiě xīnwén.

珍妮：　不过，老师 提醒 我们，不要 忘了 安全 使用 手机。

Zhēnnī:　Búguò, lǎoshī tíxǐng wǒmen, búyào wàngle ānquán shǐyòng shǒujī.

山口：　杰克，你 可 别 再 过 马路 的 时候 玩儿 手机 了！

Shānkǒu:　Jiékè, nǐ kě bié zài guò mǎlù de shíhou wánr shǒujī le!

杰克：　我 这样 做过 吗？

Jiékè:　Wǒ zhèyàng zuòguo ma?

生 词 New Words

1. 完成	wánchéng	to finish
2. 作业	zuòyè	homework
3. 上网	shàngwǎng	to surf the Internet
4. 叫外卖	jiào wàimài	to order takeout
5. 睡懒觉	shuì lǎnjiào	to sleep in
6. 食堂	shítáng	canteen
7. 方便	fāngbiàn	convenient
8. 汉堡	hànbǎo	hamburger
9. 其实	qíshí	actually
10. 几乎	jīhū	almost
11. 办	bàn	to do
12. 商店	shāngdiàn	shop
13. 机票	jīpiào	air ticket
14. 礼物	lǐwù	gift
15. 变	biàn	to become
16. 越来越	yuè lái yuè	more and more
17. 懒	lǎn	lazy
18. 享受	xiǎngshòu	to enjoy
19. 现代化	xiàndàihuà	modernization; modern

20. 生活	shēnghuó	life
21. 微信	wēixìn	WeChat
22. 随时	suíshí	at any time
23. 新闻	xīnwén	news
24. 提醒	tíxǐng	to remind
25. 马路	mǎlù	road

注 释
Notes

1 “多”“多么”，副词，强调程度很高。常常用在表示较强感情的感叹句中；也可用于问句中询问程度、数量。例如：

多 or 多么 (very) is an adverb. It indicates a high degree. It is often used in exclamatory sentences with strong feelings and can also be used to ask about degree or number in questions. For example:

1. 妈妈，我多么爱你啊！
2. 你知道，我多离不开它！
3. 你多久没见到你的女朋友了？

“多”也是形容词，形容数量大。例如：

多 is also an adjective to describe a great number. For example:

1. 人们喜欢的东西多种多样。
2. 你穿的衣服太多了！

2 “其实”，副词，申明事实或真相。有时，还表示前后的转折。例如：

其实 (actually) is an adverb. It indicates the fact or truth and sometimes shows a turn in the course of events. For example:

1. 你说他很会享受生活，其实他只知道吃汉堡包，喝可口可乐。
2. 她其实只是一个小女孩，想法很简单。
3. 他说要请我吃饭，其实他一分钱也没有。

3 “越来越……”表示程度随时间的推移而变化。例如：

越来越…… refers to the change of degree over time. For example:

1. 天气越来越热。
2. 我的汉语越来越好。
3. 越来越多的人用手机买东西。

补充生词 Additional New Words

1. 操场	cāochǎng	playground
2. 旁边	pángbiān	side
3. 老家	lǎojiā	hometown
4. 智能	zhìnéng	intelligent
5. 注意	zhùyì	to pay attention to

练习 Exercises

一、替换练习。

Substitution drills.

A：请问附近有银行吗？

B：有。

A：在哪儿？

B：学校里边。

商店	操场旁边
书店	宿舍前边
咖啡馆	马路对面
鲜花店	咖啡馆旁边

A：我很久没有见到安娜了。
B：有多久了？
A：三个星期了吧。
B：那你有空儿就去看看她吧！

吃家里的	饭菜	一年	回老家去
去	旅行	半年	出去玩儿玩儿
看	电影	两年	去电影院
见到	妈妈	一年多	回国

A：你认识珍妮多久了？
B：快一年了。
A：发现她有什么变化吗？
B：她变得越来越漂亮了。

来	北京	美丽
到	中国	现代化
买	手机	慢

二、把下面的词组成句子。

Rearrange the following words into sentences.

1. 外卖　每天　他　都　几乎　叫
2. 越来越　变　漂亮　她　得　了
3. 上网　常常　手机　他　看电影　用
4. 人们　会　越来越　现在　生活　享受　了
5. 微信　朋友　我　很　用　了　新　认识　多

三、完成对话。

Complete the following dialogues.

A：老师提醒我们＿＿＿＿＿＿＿＿＿＿＿＿。
B：有什么不安全？
A：＿＿＿＿＿＿＿＿＿＿。
B：是很危险，老师提醒得很对。

A：你去食堂吃饭吗？
B：________________。
A：你不饿吗？
B：我饿了，__________。

A：我想吃汉堡了。
B：________________？
A：附近没有汉堡店。
B：________________。
A：叫外卖？你提醒得对，我这就打电话。

四、选择“多”或“多么”，填在下面句子中适当的地方。

Fill 多 or 多么 in the appropriate places of the following sentences.

1. 不管你忙，你都要注意休息。
2. 你这么漂亮，我妈妈见了不知有喜欢！
3. 我们年不见了，今天见到你真高兴！
4. 你想不到，他家有钱。
5. 他当经理了，现在忙了。
6. 开车玩儿手机，有危险，你知道吗？
7. 你知道长安街有长吗？
8. 你看，今天的天气好！

五、模仿例句说话。

Make sentences following the example.

例句：换了智能手机，我变得越来越懒了。

1. 经理	忙
2. 蛋糕	胖
3. 新闻	了解中国
4. 天气冷	叫外卖

例句：老师提醒我们，使用手机要注意安全。

1. 完成作业
2. 低头玩儿手机
3. 记住要发票
4. 不要迟到

六、说说你使用手机时发生的有趣故事，或者你听说的一个关于手机的故事。

Tell an interesting story when you used your mobile phone or a story you heard about a mobile phone.

七、读拼音，写汉字。

Read the following passage in *pinyin*, and then write it out in Chinese characters.

Qíngrén Jié nà tiān, bàba, māma dàizhe háizi qù gōngyuán wánr. Bàba gěi māma hé háizi pāile hěn duō zhàopiàn. Gōngyuán li rén yuè lái yuè duō, bù zhī shénme shíhou, háizi bújiàn le. Bàba náchū shǒujī, gěi biérén kàn háizi de zhàopiàn, qǐng dàjiā bāngmáng zhǎo. Hěn kuài, tā jiù zhǎodào háizi le。

19

第十九课　她怎么了（一）

Lesson 19　What's the Matter with Her (Ⅰ)

课　文
Text

在课上　Zài Kè Shang

王　老师：同学们，　早上　好！
Wáng lǎoshī: Tóngxuémen, zǎoshang hǎo!

学生们：　老师　早上　好！
Xuéshengmen: Lǎoshī zǎoshang hǎo!

王　老师：同学们　都　来　了　吗？
Wáng lǎoshī: Tóngxuémen dōu lái le ma?

珍妮：　安娜　和　杰克　没有　来。
Zhēnnī: Ānnà hé Jiékè méiyǒu lái.

王　老师：他们　怎么　了？
Wáng lǎoshī: Tāmen zěnme le?

珍妮：　安娜　病　了，杰克　陪　她　去　医院　了。
Zhēnnī: Ānnà bìng le, Jiékè péi tā qù yīyuàn le.

王　老师：什么　病？
Wáng lǎoshī: Shénme bìng?

珍妮：　可能　是　感冒　了，她　说　很　不　舒服。
Zhēnnī: Kěnéng shì gǎnmào le, tā shuō hěn bù shūfu.

王　老师：发烧　吗？　量　体温　了　没有？
Wáng lǎoshī: Fāshāo ma? Liáng tǐwēn le méiyǒu?

珍妮：　　量 了。38.5℃。
Zhēnnī:　　Liáng le. 38.5℃.

王 老师：　啊，烧 得不低。咳嗽 吗？
Wáng lǎoshī: Ā, shāo de bù dī. Késou ma?

珍妮：　　不咳嗽，嗓子 也不疼，可 总 说 口渴。
Zhēnnī:　　Bù késou, sǎngzi yě bù téng, kě zǒng shuō kǒu kě.

王 老师：　应该 多喝 水。
Wáng lǎoshī: Yīnggāi duō hē shuǐ.

珍妮：　　那可不行！她 拉肚子。
Zhēnnī:　　Nà kě bùxíng! Tā lā dùzi.

王 老师：　拉肚子就 更 得 多 喝 水 了。
Wáng lǎoshī: Lā dùzi jiù gèng děi duō hē shuǐ le.

珍妮：　　那不 更 要 拉肚子 了 吗？
Zhēnnī:　　Nà bú gèng yào lā dùzi le ma?

王 老师：　哦，不会 的。
Wáng lǎoshī: Ò, bú huì de.

山口：　　我 想，她不 一定 是 感冒 了，很 可能 是 吃坏了 肚子。
Shānkǒu:　　Wǒ xiǎng, tā bù yídìng shì gǎnmào le, hěn kěnéng shì chīhuàile dùzi.

王 老师：　现在 上课 吧，下课 以后，我们 去 看看 她。
Wáng lǎochī: Xiànzài chàngkè ba, xiàkè yǐhòu, wǒmen qù kànkan tā.

生词 New Words

1. 病　　bìng　　ill, sick; disease
2. 陪　　péi　　to accompany
3. 医院　　yīyuàn　　hospital
4. 可能　　kěnéng　　maybe

5. 感冒	gǎnmào	to catch a cold
6. 舒服	shūfu	to feel well; comfortable
7. 发烧	fāshāo	to run a fever, to have a temperature
8. 量	liáng	to measure
9. 体温	tǐwēn	(body) temperature
10.（摄氏）度	(shèshì) dù	degree centigrade, Celsius
11. 低	dī	low
12. 咳嗽	késou	to cough
13. 嗓子	sǎngzi	throat, larynx
14. 疼	téng	ache, pain, sore
15. 口	kǒu	mouth, opening
16. 渴	kě	thirsty
17. 水	shuǐ	water
18. 拉	lā	to pull, to drag, to empty the bowels
19. 肚子	dùzi	belly, abdomen, stomach
20. 更	gèng	still more, even more, further
21. 坏	huài	bad, harmful
22. 下课	xiàkè	to finish class, to dismiss class

注释 Notes

1 “可能”，助动词，表示估计，不很确定。例如：

可能 is an auxiliary verb which implies estimation and uncertainty. For example:

1. 他可能没有上班。
2. 他没有钱，他爸爸可能有钱。
3. 这种车可能很贵。
4. A：这花儿她会喜欢吗？
   B：可能吧。

2 “可”“可是”，都是连词。说话人先提出一个肯定的事实，然后用“可”或“可是”转折，引出与前面相反的意思，说话人强调的是后一层意思。例如：

Both 可 and 可是 are conjunctions. The speaker first mentions a certain fact, and then uses 可 or 可是 as a turn to introduce a statement contrary to the above-mentioned fact. What the speaker stresses is the latter. For example:

1. 这衣服真漂亮，可是价钱太贵了。
2. 我想你不会来，可你还是来了。
3. 他是个什么样的人，你不知道，可我知道。
4. 我已经是大人了，可爸爸妈妈还当我是个孩子。

“可”，也是副词，表示强调，重读时还有夸张的意味。例如：

Both 可 is also an adverb, indicating emphasis. When it is stressed, it implies exaggeration. For example:

1. 你可真坏！
2. 你可不能这样做！
3. 他可是一个好人！
4. 商店的人可多啦！

“可”用在感叹盼望的事情或某种愿望已经实现时，有“终于”的意思。例如：

可 is used in exclamation to express that an expected thing or a wish has "finally" come true. For example:

1. 离家三年了，今天可回家了！
2. 大家等你半天了，你可来了！
3. 今天，我可找到工作啦！
4. 哈，这下我可有钱了！

3 “更”，副词，用于比较，表示程度高，有进一步加深的意思。例如：

更, as an adverb, is used in comparison to indicate a higher degree, with the implication of further deepening. For example:

1. 最近几年，北京更漂亮了。

2. 这个咖啡厅的顾客多了，东西也更贵了。
3. 她去年就学得不错，今年学得更好了。
4. 他现在的汉语说得更好了。

“更”还可用于比较几种事物，表示几种事物中某种事物最突出，最值得特别提出来。例如：

更 can also be used for the comparison of several things, indicating that among those things, one of them is the most outstanding and worth mentioning. For example:

1. 她爱吃苹果、葡萄，更爱吃西瓜。
2. 他不会忘了同学、同事、朋友，更不会忘了老师。
3. 小王想当老师，也想当医生，可更想当公司大老板。

补充生词 Additional New Words

1. 华氏温度	Huáshì wēndù	Fahrenheit
2. 请假	qǐngjià	to ask for leave
3. 迟到	chídào	to be late

练习 Exercises

一、替换练习。

Substitution drills.

A：你怎么了？
B：我有点儿不舒服。

感冒	发烧	拉肚子

A：你量体温了没有？
B：量了。
A：多少度？
B：36.5℃。
A：你不发烧。

36℃	不烧
37.5℃	有点儿低烧
40.6℃	烧得不低

A：谁陪安娜去医院了？
B：杰克陪安娜去医院了。

谢文	邮局	小王
朱丽亚	买西瓜	马克
山口	银行	珍妮
杰克	旅行	他的中国朋友

二、把下面的词组成句子。

Rearrange the following words into sentences.

1. 我　你　陪　买　去　东西
2. 今天　来　谁　没　上课
3. 我　已经　感冒　了　好　的
4. 别　肚子　坏　吃　了
5. 我们　看看　去　她　吧

三、完成对话。

Complete the following dialogues.

A：他今天为什么又请假了？
B：________________。

A：你今天上课迟到了吗？
B：________________。

A：你要是感冒了，会去医院吗？
B：________________。

A：发烧时你喝水还是喝茶？
B：________________。

四、指出下列各句中"可"的不同含义。

Point out the different meanings of 可 in the following sentences.

1. 你这么说，她可真要生气了。
2. 等了三个小时，他可来了。
3. 他汉语说得可好了。
4. 老师病了，可还是给我们上课。
5. 他喝了很多水，可还是口渴。
6. 要学好汉语可不容易。

五、指出下列各句中"更"的不同含义。

Point out the different meanings of 更 in the following sentences.

1. 他更有钱了。
2. 他抽烟后嗓子更疼了。
3. 经理喜欢喝咖啡，也喜欢喝啤酒，更喜欢喝中国茶。
4. 公司去年生意好，今年生意更好。
5. 他想当老板，更想当大老板。

六、模仿例句说话。

Make sentences following the example.

例句：她不一定是感冒，很可能是吃坏了肚子。

1. 有事　　病了
2. 去医院　　回家了
3. 不想买　　没有钱
4. 不想帮助你　　不能帮助你

例句：拉肚子就更得多喝水了。

1. 说得不好　　多练习
2. 发烧　　多喝水
3. 不会挑水果　　多问
4. 请别人帮助　　有礼貌

七、会话练习。

Situational conversation.

情景：A 学生不能上课，向教师请假，并说明为什么。

Scene: Student A cannot come to class. He wants to ask the teacher for leave, and explains his reason.

八、读拼音，写汉字。

Read the following passage in *pinyin* and then write it out in Chinese characters.

Yì tiān, lǎoshī shàngkè de shíhou, wèn tóngxuémen shì bú shì dōu lái le. Shānkǒu shuō Ānnà méiyǒu lái, kěshì yě méiyǒu qǐngjià. Lǎoshī wèn tā wèi shénme méi lái shàngkè. Zhēnnī shuō Ānnà bìng le, kěnéng shì gǎnmào le. Kě Shānkǒu shuō, bù yídìng shì gǎnmào, hěn kěnnéng shì chīhuàile dùzi. Lǎoshī shuō, xiàkè yǐhòu, dàjiā yìqǐ qù kànkan Ānnà.

20

第二十课 她怎么了（二）

Lesson 20 What's the Matter with Her (Ⅱ)

课 文

Text

在课外 Zài Kè Wài

钱 富成：先生， 你们 是 去 旅行 吗？
Qián Fùchéng: Xiānsheng, nǐmen shì qù lǚxíng ma?
杰克： 是 啊。你 呢？
Jiékè: Shì a. Nǐ ne?
钱 富成： 出差， 做 生意。
Qián Fùchéng: Chūchāi, zuò shēngyi.
杰克： 做 生意？ 怎么 不 坐 飞机？
Jiékè: Zuò shēngyi? Zěnme bú zuò fēijī?
钱 富成： 吃 点儿 苦，节省 点儿 经费。
Qián Fùchéng: Chī diǎnr kǔ, jiéshěng diǎnr jīngfèi.
杰克： 可 火车 太 慢。 生意人 最 讲究 的 就 是 时间。
Jiékè: Kě huǒchē tài màn. Shēngyirén zuì jiǎngjiu de jiù shì shíjiān.
钱 富成： 是 啊。时间 就是 金钱 嘛！
Qián Fùchéng: Shì a. Shíjiān jiù shì jīnqián ma!
杰克： 可是……
Jiékè: Kěshì…

钱富成： 没 关系，今天 是 休息日。
Qián Fùchéng: Méi guānxi, jīntiān shì xiūxirì.

杰克： 对了，大家 都 不 上班。
Jiékè: Duìle, dàjiā dōu bú shàngbān.

钱富成： 你的 朋友 怎么 一路 都 在 睡觉？
Qián Fùchéng: Nǐ de péngyou zěnme yílù dōu zài shuìjiào?

杰克： 她 有点儿 不 舒服。
Jiékè: Tā yǒudiǎnr bù shūfu.

钱富成： 怎么 光 睡觉，不 吃 点儿 药？
Qián Fùchéng: Zěnme guāng shuìjiào, bù chī diǎnr yào?

杰克： 上 火车 的 时候 还 好好儿 的，昨天 晚上 才 开始 的。我们 想 下了 火车 去 买 药。
Jiékè: Shàng huǒchē de shíhou hái hǎohāor de, zuótiān wǎnshang cái kāishǐ de. Wǒmen xiǎng xiàle huǒchē qù mǎi yào.

钱富成： 啊？你们 等等，我 去 找 大夫。
Qián Fùchéng: Á? Nǐmen děngdeng, wǒ qù zhǎo dàifu.

钱富成： 大夫 来 了。
Qián Fùchéng: Dàifu lái le.

大夫： 你 怎么 了？
Dàifu: Nǐ zěnme le?

安娜： 我 头 疼 得 厉害。
Ānnà: Wǒ tóu téng de lìhai.

大夫： 哦，你 正在 发烧 呢，量 一 量 体温 吧。
Dàifu: Ò, nǐ zhèngzài fāshāo ne, liáng yi liáng tǐwēn ba.

大夫： 把 体温表 给 我。40℃，烧 得 厉害。让 我 看看 嗓子。
Dàifu: Bǎ tǐwēnbiǎo gěi wǒ. 40℃, shāo de lìhai. Ràng wǒ kànkan sǎngzi.

杰克： 有 什么 问题 吗？
Jiékè: Yǒu shénme wèntí ma?

大夫：　嗓子 发炎 了。
Dàifu:　Sǎngzi fāyán le.

杰克：　要 打针 吗？她 怕 打针！
Jiékè:　Yào dǎzhēn ma? Tā pà dǎzhēn!

大夫：　先 吃点儿 退烧药 吧。一 次 吃 两 片，四 小时 吃 一 次。
Dàifu:　Xiān chī diǎnr tuìshāoyào ba. yí cì chī liǎng piàn, sì xiǎoshí chī yí cì.

安娜：　大夫，我 的 病 要紧 吗？
Ānnà:　Dàifu, wǒ de bìng yàojǐn ma?

大夫：　下了 车，去 医院 好好儿 检查 检查 吧。
Dàifu:　Xiàle chē, qù yīyuàn hǎohāor jiǎnchá jiǎnchá ba.

安娜：　啊，可 别 住院！
Ānnà:　À, kě bié zhùyuàn!

生词 New Words

1. 出差	chūchāi	to go on a business trip, to travel on official business
2. 飞机	fēijī	aircraft, plane
3. 苦	kǔ	bitter, hardship; to cause sb. to suffer
4. 节省	jiéshěng	to economize, to save, to use sparingly
5. 经费	jīngfèi	fund, outlay
6. 火车	huǒchē	train
7. 慢	màn	slow
8. 讲究	jiǎngjiu	to stress, to be particular about, to pay attention to
9. 时间	shíjiān	time
10. 金钱	jīnqián	money
11. 嘛	ma	*a particle indicating that sth. is obvious*

12. 休息	xiūxi	to rest
13. 一路	yílù	all the way, throughout the journey
14. 睡觉	shuìjiào	to sleep
15. 光	guāng	only, alone, merely
16. 药	yào	medicine
17. 大夫	dàifu	doctor
18. 把	bǎ	*used when the object is placed before the verb*
19. 体温表	tǐwēnbiǎo	thermometer
20. 厉害	lìhai	severe, terrible, harsh
21. 发炎	fāyán	to get inflamed
22. 打针	dǎzhēn	to give (have) an injection
23. 怕	pà	to fear, to be afraid of
24. 退	tuì	to move back, to decline, to fade, to give back
25. 片	piàn	tablet, slice
26. 要紧	yàojǐn	serious, important
27. 检查	jiǎnchá	to check up, to inspect, to examine
28. 住院	zhùyuàn	to be hospitalized

专名 Proper Noun

钱富成	Qián Fùchéng	Qian Fucheng

注释 Notes

1 “时间”与“时候”，都是名词，表示有起点、有终点的一段时间，也可表示时间里的某一点。但是这两个词，也有一点儿区别。“时候”，多用于口语；“时间”用于口语时，多用来说明时间点和较确定的、具体的时间。在书面语体中，表达时间概念时，不适宜用“时候”，而要用“时间”。“时候”还可以说“当……的时候”，而“时间”不这么说。例如：

Both 时间 and 时候 are nouns indicating a duration of time with a starting point and an ending point. They can also express a point of time. However, there is a subtle difference between these two words, 时候 is more frequently used in spoken Chinese. When 时间 is used in spoken Chinese, it more often than not expresses a point of time or a definite or concrete time. In written Chinese, we should use 时间 rather than 时候 to express the concept of time. We can also say 当……的时候, but 时间 cannot be used in this way. For example:

1. 你今天用了多长时间做练习？
2. 火车什么时候到北京？
3. 火车到北京的时间是十二点零五分。
4. 她小时候是个很漂亮的女孩儿。
5. 当他想起爸爸妈妈的时候，他就想回家。
6. 时间在一分一秒地过去，还是不知道飞机哪儿出了问题。

2 “把”，做介词时，构成“把”字句，是现代汉语里常用的句式，也是外国人较难掌握的句型，需要特别注意学习。“把”字句中的主要动词一般都是及物动词，是能支配后面的宾语的。“把”字后的名词是这个主要动词的宾语，用“把”字提到动词的前面去了。动词后还应有相关成分，不能只剩下一个单独的动词。例如，不能说“把门关”，要说“把门关上”。充当宾语的名词，所指事物必须是确定的，已知的。例如：

把, when used as a preposition, constructs a 把-sentence, which is a common sentence pattern in modern Chinese, and which is difficult for foreigners to master. Hence it deserves special attention. The main verb in the 把-sentence is generally a transitive verb, which can govern the object that follows. The noun after the character 把 is the object of this main verb, and 把 brings it forward to a place before the verb. The verb cannot stand alone either, that is, there must be some related elements after it. For instance, for “close the door”, we cannot say 把门关, but have to say 把门关上. The noun functioning as the object must be something definite, something that is already known. For example:

1. 请你把这本书给他。——请你给他这本书。
2. 我把药吃下去了。——我吃了药了。
3. 他把“四”念成（niànchéng）“十”了。——“四”他念成“十”了。

4. 你把我忘了。——你忘了我了。
5. 我把练习做完了。——我做完练习了。
6. 我把肚子吃坏了。——我吃坏肚子了。

补充生词
Additional New Word

双休日　　shuāngxiūrì　　two-day weekend

练　习
Exercises

一、替换练习。
Substitution drills.

A：你们是去旅行吗？
B：不，我们是去出差。

火车站	飞机场
北京大学	清华大学
找朋友	看大夫
学习	买水果

A：你的头疼厉害吗？
B：很厉害，疼得睡不着觉。

感冒	几天高烧不退
护士	她天天要我打针吃药
医生	他不让我出院
老板	他不让我休息

二、把下面的词组成句子。

Rearrange the following words into sentences.

1. 你　出差　哪儿　去
2. 她　能　吃苦　不
3. 你　应该　经费　节省　点儿
4. 坐　帮助　能　中国　火车　了解　我
5. 我　要紧　有　事　的

三、完成对话。

Complete the following dialogues.

A：你旅行的时候生过病吗？
B：________________________。

A：________________________？
B：我怕打针。

A：你昨天晚上睡得怎么样？
B：________________________。

A：你带钱了吗？
B：对不起，____________。

A：________________________？
B：我在家休息。

四、在下列各句中填写“时间”或“时候”，并想想为什么。

Fill in the blanks with 时间 or 时候 and think about the reason.

1. 生病的______最想家。
2. 要是你想学习就会有______。
3. 有钱的______不要忘了没钱的朋友。

4. 坐飞机可以节省______，可没有坐火车有意思。
5. 请别人帮助的______，应该有礼貌。
6. ______不多了，可考试我还没准备好。
7. 开车的______不能打电话。
8. 上课的______好好上课，下课的______好好休息，这才是会学习的好学生。

五、把下列各句改成“把”字句。

Rewrite the following sentences into 把-sentences.

1. 请系好安全带。
2. 这个字你写错了。
3. 你忘了她吧。
4. 请你给我体温表。
5. 这杯酒我已经喝完了。

六、把下列“把”字句改成不带“把”字的陈述句。

Rewrite the following 把-sentences into declarative sentences without 把.

1. 我把她送回家了。
2. 我把发票给顾客了。
3. 哥哥把这本书看完了。
4. 秘书把工作安排好了。
5. 我把给妈妈留言的事忘了。

七、模仿例句说话。

Make sentences following the example.

例句：生意人最讲究的就是时间。

1. 生病	最麻烦的
2. 旅行	最怕的
3. 学汉语	最要紧的
4. 老师	最喜欢的

八、会话练习。

Situational conversation.

情景：陪生病的朋友去医院看病，大夫问病、检查，你或朋友回答。

Scene: Accompany your sick friend to see a doctor. The doctor inquires about the symptoms and gives your friend a check-up. You or your friend answers the doctor's questions.

九、读拼音，写汉字。

Read the following passage in *pinyin* and then write it out in Chinese characters.

Qián jīnglǐ chūchāi, zài huǒchē shang rènshile liúxuéshēng Jiékè hé Ānnà. Tāmen yílù shang shuōle hěn duō huà. Jékè bù lǐjiě, Qián jīnglǐ chūchāi zuò shēngyi, wèi shénme bú zuò fēijī. Qián jīnglǐ shuō, zhè liǎng tiān shì shuāngxiūrì, dàjiā dōu bú shàngbān, zuò huǒchē, bú huì wùshì, hái kěyǐ jiéshěng jīngfèi.

21

第二十一课　是谁的错（一）

Lesson 21　Whose Fault Is It (I)

课　文

Text

在课上　Zài Kè Shang

杰克：　　老师，您好！
Jiékè:　　Lǎoshī, nínhǎo!

王　老师：你 好！今天 你 怎么 又 迟到 了？
Wáng lǎoshī: Nǐ hǎo! Jīntiān nǐ zěnme yòu chídào le?

杰克：　　我 没 迟到 呀！看，我的 手表 现在 才 七 点 五十。我 还 早 到 了 呢！
Jiékè:　　Wǒ méi chídào ya! Kàn, wǒ de shǒubiǎo xiànzài cái qī diǎn wǔshí. Wǒ hái zǎo dào le ne!

珍妮：　　才 七 点 五十？都 八 点 一刻 了！晚了 一 刻钟 了！
Zhēnnī:　　Cái qī diǎn wǔshí? Dōu bā diǎn yí kè le! Wǎnle yí kèzhōng le!

杰克：　　怎么 会？一定 是 你的 表 错 了。
Jiékè:　　Zěnme huì? Yídìng shì nǐ de biǎo cuò le.

王　老师：好 了，坐下 吧，把 书 拿 出来。
Wáng lǎoshī: Hǎo le, zuòxia ba, bǎ shū ná chūlái.

杰克：　　哎呀，糟糕 了！
Jiékè:　　Āiyā, zāogāo le!

珍妮：　你 又 拿错 书 了，是不是？
Zhēnnī:　Nǐ yòu nácuò shū le, shì bú shì?

杰克：　不是 张 老师 的 听力 课 吗？怎么 是 王 老师 上 课？
Jiékè:　Bú shì Zhāng lǎoshī de tīnglì kè ma? Zěnme shì Wáng lǎoshī shàng kè?

珍妮：　这 节 课 是 王 老师 的 口语 课！
Zhēnnī:　Zhè jié kè shì Wáng lǎoshī de kǒuyǔ kè!

杰克：　我 刚才 走进 教室 就 觉得 奇怪！今天 星期 几？
Jiékè:　Wǒ gāngcái zǒujìn jiàoshì jiù juéde qíguài! Jīntiān xīngqī jǐ?

珍妮：　今天 星期 二！
Zhēnnī:　Jīntiān xīngqī èr!

杰克：　星期 二？看，我 的 手表 是 星期 一。
Jiékè:　Xīngqī èr? Kàn, wǒ de shǒubiǎo shì xīngqī yī.

珍妮：　我 说 你 昨天 怎么 没来 上课 呢，原来 昨天 是 你 的 星期天 啊！
Zhēnnī:　Wǒ shuō nǐ zuótiān zěnme méi lái shàngkè ne, yuánlái zuótiān shì nǐ de xīngqītiān a!

杰克：　我 可 没 休息，我 打工 挣 钱 去 了！
Jiékè:　Wǒ kě méi xiūxi, wǒ dǎgōng zhèng qián qù le!

王 老师：你们 俩 在 说 什么 呢？
Wáng lǎoshī: Nǐmen liǎ zài shuō shénme ne?

珍妮：　杰克 以为 今天 是 星期 一，所以 他 只 带了 听力 课本。
Zhēnnī:　Jiékè yǐwéi jīntiān shì xīngqī yī, suǒyǐ tā zhǐ dàile tīnglì kèběn.

杰克：　老师，这 不 能 怪 我，是 表 错 了。我 保证，明天 它 不会 再 错 了。
Jiékè:　Lǎoshī, zhè bù néng guài wǒ, shì biǎo cuò le. Wǒ bǎozhèng, míngtiān tā bú huì zài cuò le.

山口：　如果　明天　你　上课　再　迟到，又　该　怪　谁　呢？
Shānkǒu:　Rúguǒ míngtiān nǐ shàngkè zài chídào, yòu gāi guài shéi ne?

杰克：　是　啊，又　该　怪　谁　呢？　怪　我　自己？　哦，不……
Jiékè:　Shì a, yòu gāi guài shéi ne? Guài wǒ zìjǐ? Ò, bù…

生词 New Words

1. 手表	shǒubiǎo	wrist watch
2. 早	zǎo	early
3. 晚	wǎn	late, evening, night
4. 拿	ná	to hold, to take
5. 出来	chūlái	*used after a verb indicating the motion towards the speaker or the completion of an action*
6. 哎呀	āiyā	*an interjection expressing surprise or complaint*
7. 糟糕	zāogāo	bad, terrible
8. 听力	tīnglì	listening comprehension, hearing
9. 节	jié	*a measure word for classes*
10. 口语	kǒuyǔ	spoken language, oral (class)
11. 觉得	juéde	to feel, to think
12. 奇怪	qíguài	strange, odd
13. 原来	yuánlái	original; actually; as it turns out
14. 打工	dǎgōng	to do a temporary work, to work as an employee
15. 挣钱	zhèng qián	to earn money, to make money
16. 俩	liǎ	two (*usually used in spoken Chinese*)

17. 以为	yǐwéi	to think, to believe, to consider
18. 所以	suǒyǐ	as a result, therefore
19. 带	dài	to take, to bring, to carry
20. 课本	kèběn	textbook
21. 怪	guài	to blame
22. 保证	bǎozhèng	to pledge, to guarantee, to ensure
23. 它	tā	it
24. 如果	rúguǒ	if, in case

注释

Notes

1 “都”，副词，表示总括全部。例如：

都, an adverb, expresses that all are included. For example:

1. 我们都来了。
2. 我们互相都认识。
3. 我们都学习汉语。

“都……了”，强调时间迫近或情况早已存在。“都”要轻读，重音在“都”的后边。例如：

都……了 emphasizes that the time is drawing near or the situation has long existed. Here 都 should be pronounced lightly, with the stress falling on what comes after 都. For example:

1. 快跑，火车都进站了。
2. 他都生气了，你还说个不停！
3. 我们约好九点钟见面，都十点了，他还不来。
4. 她都快工作了，还像一个小孩儿。

2 “我说……呢”或者“我说呢”，表示忽然醒悟、明白。后面常用“原来”带出“醒悟”到的是什么。例如：

我说……呢 or 我说呢 expresses a sudden realization or understanding. It is often followed by 原来 to introduce what has been understood. For example:

1. 我说你怎么会拉肚子呢，原来是你吃多了羊肉串！
2. 我说呢，他怎么来晚了，原来是表坏了。
3. 我说呢，他的口语这么好，原来他有很多中国朋友。

3 “原来”，副词，表示说话人发现了以前不知道的情况，或对某种情况有所醒悟。例如：

原来, as an adverb, indicates that the speaker has discovered something he didn't know before, or that he has come to realize something. For example:

1. 我说是谁呢，原来是你啊！
2. 我以为你知道呢，原来你也不知道。
3. 他出门就叫出租车，原来他打工赚了很多钱。
4. 大家都奇怪他今天为什么没来上班，原来是病了。

4 “所以”，连词，用来表示因果关系，或推理和结论的关系。例如：

所以, as a conjunction, expresses a cause-effect, or reasoning-conclusion relationship. For example:

1. 我没有工作，所以我没有钱。
2. 我得到了很多人的帮助，所以我的汉语学得很好。
3. 他太容易相信人，所以他常常吃苦头。
4. 我不了解她，所以我不知道她以后想做什么。

5 “如果”，表示假设，用在前一分句，有时后面还可加助词“的话”；后一分句常与“就、也、那么”等词相呼应，表示在前一种假设情况下出现的结果。例如：

如果 (if) expresses a supposition. It is used in the first clause. Sometimes it can be followed by the particle 的话. The second clause often echoes with such words as 就 (then), 也 (too) or 那么 (then), expressing an outcome resulting from that supposition. For example:

1. 如果你去（的话），我也去。

2. 如果便宜（的话），我就买。
3. 你如果相信他，那可就糟糕了！
4. 如果你觉得那样做不好，就不要那样做。

补充生词 Additional New Words

1. 站	zhàn	station, stop; to stand
2. 见面	jiànmiàn	to meet, to see
3. 羊肉串	yángròuchuàn	mutton cubes roasted on a skewer, kabob
4. 赚钱	zhuàn qián	to make money, to make a profit

练习 Exercises

一、替换练习。

Substitution drills.

A：哎呀，糟了！
B：你怎么了？
A：我拿错书了。
B：真的？以后可别再拿错书了！

看	表
写	汉字
认	人
叫	名字

A：你今天不是有课吗？怎么还睡觉？

B：我好像有点儿不舒服。

休息	来上班了	一个人在家没意思
要出差	还在这儿	有了新的安排
有约会	没买鲜花	已经取消了约会
要去看女朋友	不早点儿走	想试试她会不会等我

二、把下面的词组成句子。

Rearrange the following words into sentences.

1. 上课　迟到　你　了
2. 没有　今天　我们　口语课
3. 我们　哪儿　听力课　在　上
4. 你　才　怎么　呢　现在　来
5. 我　没有　保证　他　你　忘记

三、完成对话。

Complete the following dialogues.

A：______________________？

B：不会迟到，现在还早呢，才七点四十五！

A：你的表不会错吧？

B：______________________。

A：谁拿了我的书？

B：______________________吧？

A：我问小王了，他说他没拿我的书。

B：______________________。

A：经理，对不起，我昨天没有来上班。
B：________________________？
A：________________________。
B：我说呢，原来是病了。

A：在你们国家，打工赚钱吗？
B：________________________。
A：________________________？
B：在饭店当服务员一个小时是五美元。

四、读出下列各句的重音，说明各句中“都”字的含义。

Read the following sentences and get the stresses right. Then explain the meaning of 都 in each sentence.

1. 大家都以为你不来了，你怎么又来了？
2. 没问题了，钱都兑换好了。
3. 你都发烧了，还不吃药？
4. 大家都觉得奇怪，老板怎么什么都知道了。
5. 去中国旅行要带什么，我都告诉他了。
6. 你都打工挣钱了，还说没钱请朋友喝啤酒。
7. 都什么时候了，你还在睡觉？

五、模仿例句说话。

Make sentences following the example.

例句：我说你昨天怎么没来上课呢，原来昨天是你的星期天啊！

1. 现在有钱了	打工挣钱
2. 了解她	你们是朋友
3. 送鲜花给她	她的生日
4. 还睡觉	病了
5. 高兴	妈妈来了

例句：如果你明天再迟到，以后就别来上班了。

1. 有时间	去看你
2. 不舒服	看医生
3. 路上堵车	糟糕了
4. 相信我	交个朋友
5. 有钱	帮助她们

六、会话练习。

Situational conversation.

情景：去约会的时候，你向对方解释为什么去晚了。

Scene: Explain why you are late for the appointment.

七、读拼音，写汉字。

Read the following passage in *pinyin*, and then write it out in Chinese characters.

Jiékè chángcháng shàngkè chídào, hái chángcháng nácuò shū. Wèi shénme? Jiékè zǒngshì shuō, shì tā de shǒubiǎo bù hǎo. Tā shàngkè chídào, nácuò shū, bù néng guài tā, yīnggāi guài shǒubiǎo. Jiékè wèi shénme zhème xiǎng ne? Zhēn qíguài!

22

第二十二课　是谁的错（二）

Lesson 22　Whose Fault Is It (II)

课　文

Text

在课外　Zài Kè Wài

杰克：　小姐，从　上海　来的14次　特快列车　什么时候　到？
Jiékè:　Xiǎojie, cóng Shànghǎi lái de 14 cì tèkuài lièchē shénme shíhou dào?

小姐：　九点　零一分　到　站。现在　才七　点　半，还　早　呢！
Xiǎojie:　Jiǔ diǎn líng yī fēn dào zhàn. Xiànzài cái qī diǎn bàn, hái zǎo ne!

杰克：　什么？　才七　点　半？
Jiékè:　Shénme? Cái qī diǎn bàn?

小姐：　是呀，你看，这大楼　上　的钟，不是七　点　半吗？
Xiǎojie:　Shì ya, nǐ kàn, zhè dà lóu shang de zhōng, bú shì qī diǎn bàn ma?

杰克：　不对！我　刚　对过　表，现在　是八　点　半，一定　是大　楼　上　的　钟　慢　了。
Jiékè:　Búduì! Wǒ gāng duìguo biǎo, xiànzài shì bā diǎn bàn, yídìng shì dà lóu shang de zhōng màn le.

小姐：　那 怎么 会？是 你 的 表 快 了。
Xiǎojie: Nà zěnme huì? Shì nǐ de biǎo kuài le.

杰克：　是 吗？这 该死 的 表，害 得 我 这么 早 就 起床，现在 还 得 等 一个 多 小时。
Jiékè: Shì ma? Zhè gāisǐ de biǎo, hài de wǒ zhème zǎo jiù qǐchuáng, xiànzài hái děi děng yí gè duō xiǎoshí.

小姐：　你 是 来 接 人 的？
Xiǎojie: Nǐ shì lái jiē rén de?

杰克：　是，接 上海 来 的 一 个 朋友。
Jiékè: Shì, jiē Shànghǎi lái de yí gè péngyou.

小姐：　你 的 朋友 是 第一 次 来 北京？
Xiǎojie: Nǐ de péngyou shì dì-yī cì lái Běijīng?

杰克：　不，他 常 坐 火车 来 北京 出差，我 是 第一 次 来 火车站。
Jiékè: Bù, tā cháng zuò huǒchē lái Běijīng chūchā, wǒ shì dì-yī cì lái huǒchēzhàn.

小姐：　哦，这么 说，你 的 朋友 应该 来 接 你。
Xiǎojie: Ó, zhème shuō, nǐ de péngyou yīnggāi lái jiē nǐ.

杰克：　为 什么？
Jiékè: Wèi shénme?

小姐：　他 不 会 说"这 大 楼 上 的 钟 错 了！"
Xiǎojie: Tā bú huì shuō "Zhè dà lóu shang de zhōng cuò le!"

杰克：　喂，史特凡，我 在 这儿！
Jiékè: Wèi, Shǐtèfán, wǒ zài zhèr!

史特凡：嗨，杰克，见到 你 真 高兴！
Shǐtèfán: Hēi, Jiékè, jiàndào nǐ zhēn gāoxìng!

杰克：　一路 顺利？
Jiékè: Yílù shùnlì?

史特凡：一切 顺利！
Shǐtèfán: Yíqiè shùnlì!

杰克：　你 总是 一切 顺利，我 可是 常常
Jiékè: Nǐ zǒngshì yíqiè shùnlì, wǒ kě shì chángcháng

遇到 麻烦。
yùdào máfan.

史特凡： 怎么 啦？
Shǐtèfán: Zěnme la?

杰克： 这 该死 的 表，总 耽误 事！
Jiékè: Zhè gāisǐ de biǎo, zǒng dānwu shì!

史特凡： 你 的 表 怎么 了？
Shǐtèfán: Nǐ de biǎo zěnme le?

杰克： 前 几 天 太 慢，我 上课 总 迟到；今天 又 太 快，害得 我 在 这儿 等了 你 一 个 多 小时！
Jiékè: Qián jǐ tiān tài màn, wǒ shàngkè zǒng chídào; jīntiān yòu tài kuài, hài de wǒ zài zhèr děngle nǐ yí gè duō xiǎoshí!

史特凡： 哈…… 你 要 是 我 公司 的 职员，我 一定 要 开除 你！
Shǐtèfán: Hā… Nǐ yào shì wǒ gōngsī de zhíyuán, wǒ yídìng yào kāichú nǐ!

生词 New Words

1. 特快列车	tèkuài lièchē	express, express train
2. 楼	lóu	(storeyed) building
3. 该死	gāisǐ	damn it
4. 害	hài	to cause trouble to
5. 这么	zhème	so, such, this way, like this
6. 起床	qǐchuáng	to get up, to get out of bed
7. 接	jiē	to meet, to welcome
8. 第	dì	*used before numerals to form ordinal numbers*
9. 顺利	shùnlì	smooth, without a hitch

10. 一切	yíqiè	all, every, everything
11. 总是	zǒngshì	always
12. 常	cháng	often, frequently
13. 遇到	yùdào	to run into, to encounter, to come across
14. 麻烦	máfan	trouble
15. 耽误	dānwu	to delay, to hold up
16. 职员	zhíyuán	staff member
17. 开除	kāichú	to expel, to discharge

专　名　Proper Noun

史特凡	Shǐtèfán	Steven

注释 Notes

1 "从"，介词，表示起点。例如：

从 (from), a preposition, indicates the starting point. For example:

1. 你从哪儿来？
2. 我从美国来。
3. 我们从八点开始上课。
4. 从学校到北京火车站，坐出租车要半个小时。

2 "这么"，代词，指称事物的具体性状、程度，或动作的具体方式。事物的这种具体性状、程度，或动作的具体方式，是说话人和听话人都了解的。例如：

这么, a pronoun, refers to the specific characteristic or degree of something, or the mode of an action, which is known by both the speaker and hearer. For example:

1. 你怎么交了这么一个朋友！
2. 你买了这么个西瓜，真糟糕！

3. 这事儿不能这么办！
4. 你这么说，我就明白了。
5. 他这么爱你，你还不高兴？

3 “总”“总是”，副词，表示过去经常这样，很少例外，现在也还是这样。例如：

总 and 总是 are adverbs indicating that it was always like this in the past, with very few exceptions, and it remains like this now. For example:

1. 你总这样，谁还愿意跟你交朋友。
2. 他总缺钱用。
3. 他总是说假话。
4. 他总是找我的麻烦。

4 “要”，连词，表假设，只是不像“要是”，可以放在主语前边。它只能放在主语后边。例如：

要, a conjunction, indicates supposition. Unlike 要是, 要 can't occur before the subject. It is only used after the subject. For example:

1. 你要不喜欢，就别买。（不能说“要你不喜欢，就别买。”）
2. 你要不说，我怎么知道？
3. 你要不会，我可以帮助你。
4. 火车要晚点，可就糟糕了。

补充生词 Additional New Words

1. 晚点	wǎndiǎn	late, behind schedule
2. 正点	zhèngdiǎn	on time, on schedule
3. 赔钱	péiqián	to make a loss in business, to lose money
4. 航班	hángbān	flight

练　习
Exercises

一、替换练习。
Substitution drills.

A：从上海来的14次特快列车什么时候到？
B：九点零一分到。

西安	280次列车	20:25
山海关	551次列车	14:05
巴黎	CA950航班	11:45
纽约	CZ190航班	22:20

A：你是什么时候来北京的？
B：我是今年9月3日来北京的。
A：你这是第一次来北京吗？
B：不，我这是第二次来北京。

来中国	去年2月25日
去上海	1999年7月30日
去西安	2006年10月1日
去巴黎	2015年5月10日

A：你是来机场接人的吗？
B：是，我来接留学生。你也是来接人的？
A：不，我来送朋友。

朋友	老板
老板	同事
同事	我妈妈
公司总裁	同学

二、把下面的词组成句子。
Rearrange the following words into sentences.

1. 预订　我　特快列车　14次　一张　要　票　的
2. 我　机场　接　去　朋友
3. 他　坐　出差　喜欢　火车
4. 这　飞机　误点　了　班
5. 常常　我　麻烦　遇到

三、完成对话。

Complete the following dialogues.

A：你第一次来北京是什么时候？
B：________________________。

A：总是迟到的职员，公司会开除他吗？
B：________________________。

A：老板，________________？
B：你总是给公司带来麻烦，所以我要开除你。

A：你的生意做得顺利吗？
B：不，____________________。

四、模仿例句说话。

Make sentences following the example.

例句：这该死的表，总是耽误事儿！

1. 电话	占线
2. 马路	堵车
3. 司机	迟到
4. 老板	不让我休息

例句：你总是一切顺利，我可是常常遇到麻烦。

1. 有钱	缺钱
2. 赚钱	赔钱
3. 帮助别人	要别人帮助
4. 出门就打的	走路

五、用括号里的词完成句子。

Complete the following sentences with the words in the brackets.

1. 我做生意 ________________。（麻烦）
2. 要是火车晚点，________________。（糟糕）
3. 你到机场后，________________。（接）
4. 我很高兴听说，________________。（顺利）
5. 你要是遇到麻烦，________________。（打电话）
6. 你要是找他的麻烦，________________。（生气）

六、会话练习。

Situational conversation.

情景：去机场接朋友，可路上堵车。你到机场的时候，飞机早已到了，你向朋友解释，请朋友原谅。

Scene: You go to the airport to meet a friend. Because of the traffic jam, the plane arrives long before you get to the airport. You go into an explanation and apologize to your friend.

七、读拼音，写汉字。

Read the following passage in *pinyin*, and then write it out in Chinese characters.

Yì tiān, Jiékè qù huǒchēzhàn jiē pěngyou. Tā de biǎo kuài le, hài de tā děng le yí gè duō xiǎoshí. Tā de péngyou zài Shànghǎi zuò shēngyi, chángcháng lái Běijīng chūchāi. Cóng Shànghǎi lái de huǒchē zhèngdiǎn dàole Běijīng Zhàn. Jiékè jiàndào lǎopéngyou, tèbié gāoxìng, tā hěn kuài wàngle tā yùdào de máfan.

23

第二十三课 住在哪儿（一）

Lesson 23 Where Do You Live (Ⅰ)

课 文

Text

在课上 Zài Kè Shang

王 老师：杰克，你 住 在 哪儿？
Wáng lǎoshī: Jiékè, Nǐ zhù zài nǎr?

杰克： 我 住 在 学校 的 4 号 楼。
Jiékè: Wǒ zhù zài xuéxiào de 4 hào lóu.

王 老师：珍妮，你 呢？
Wáng lǎoshī: Zhēnnī, nǐ ne?

珍妮： 我 也 住 在 4 号 楼。
Zhēnnī: Wǒ yě zhù zài 4 hào lóu.

王 老师：住 几 号 房间？
Wáng lǎoshī: Zhù jǐ hào fángjiān?

珍妮： 3 层 347，杰克 住 2 层 215。
Zhēnnī: 3 céng 347, Jiékè zhù 2 céng 215.

王 老师：你们 几 个 人 住 一 个 房间？
Wáng lǎoshī: Nǐmen jǐ gè rén zhù yí gè fángjiān?

杰克： 两 个。
Jiékè: Liǎng gè.

王 老师：房间 里边 有 电话 吗？
Wáng lǎoshī: Fángjiān lǐbian yǒu diànhuà ma?

珍妮： 有 一 个，可 有 时候，同屋 打 电话，我
Zhēnnī: Yǒu yí gè, kě yǒu shíhou, tóngwū dǎ diànhuà, wǒ

就不能打了。
jiù bù néng dǎ le.

杰克：可不是嘛！
Jiékè: Kěbúshi ma!

山口：哦，那不太方便。
Shānkǒu: Ò, nà bú tài fāngbiàn.

杰克：还是山口好，住在学校外边。
Jiékè: Háishi Shānkǒu hǎo, zhù zài xuéxiào wàibian.

王老师：山口，你住哪儿？
Wáng lǎoshī: Shānkǒu, nǐ zhù nǎr?

山口：我住亚运村附近，离学校很近。
Shānkǒu: Wǒ zhù Yàyùncūn fùjìn, lí xuéxiào hěn jìn.

王老师：为什么不住学校里边？
Wáng lǎoshī: Wèi shénme bú zhù xuéxiào lǐbian?

珍妮：住学校外边，房租多贵呀！
Zhēnnī: Zhù xuéxiào wàibian, fángzū duō guì ya!

山口：我先生的公司给我们租了一套公寓，
Shānkǒu: Wǒ xiānsheng de gōngsī gěi wǒmen zūle yí tào gōngyù,

我们不付房租。
wǒmen bú fù fángzū.

珍妮：环境怎么样？
Zhēnnī: Huánjìng zěnmeyàng?

山口：很好。购物，娱乐，都很方便。
Shānkǒu: Hěn hǎo. Gòuwù, yúlè, dōu hěn fāngbiàn.

珍妮：啊，那真不错！
Zhēnnī: À, nà zhēn búcuò!

山口：欢迎你们去玩儿。这是我先生的
Shānkǒu: Huānyíng nǐmen qù wánr. Zhè shì wǒ xiānsheng de

名片，上面有地址和电话号码。
míngpiàn, shàngmiàn yǒu dìzhǐ hé diànhuà hàomǎ.

珍妮：谢谢，有空儿我们一定去拜访你们。
Zhēnnī: Xièxie, yǒu kòngr wǒmen yídìng qù bàifǎng nǐmen.

生词 New Words

1. 层	céng	floor
2. 里（边）	lǐ (bian)	in, inside, within
3. 同屋	tóngwū	roommate
4. 外（边）	wài (bian)	outside
5. 附近	fùjìn	nearby, close to
6. 近	jìn	near, close
7. 房租	fángzū	rent
8. 套	tào	*indicating series or sets of things*
9. 公寓	gōngyù	apartment, flat
10. 付	fù	to pay
11. 环境	huánjìng	environment
12. 娱乐	yúlè	recreation, entertainment
13. 名片	míngpiàn	business card
14. 上面	shàngmiàn	on the surface of, above
15. 地址	dìzhǐ	address
16. 有空儿	yǒu kòngr	to have time to spare
17. 拜访	bàifǎng	to pay a visit, to call on

专名 Proper Noun

亚运村	Yàyùncūn	Asian Games Village

注释 Notes

1 “里、外、上、下、左、右、前、后”，是表方位的名词，可以单独使用，也可以用“边”、“面”等词合起来用。例如：

里 (in), 外 (out), 上 (up), 下 (down), 左 (left), 右 (right), 前 (front) and 后 (behind) are all nouns of locality. They can be used alone or together with such words as 边 or 面. For example:

1. 房间里有三个人。
2. 安娜坐在我的右边。
3. 真糟糕，前边堵车了！
4. 请你们到外面去说话，我要睡觉了。

2 “可不”“可不是”，表示肯定、赞同，语气较强。例如：

可不 or 可不是 expresses affirmation or agreement in a rather strong tone. For example:

A：你最好早点儿预订房间。
B：可不，我也这么想！

A：现在正是上下班时间，走哪儿都堵车。
B：可不是，你说得一点儿都不错。

3 “离”，介词，由“离”组成的介词结构在句子中做状语，表示时间和空间的距离。例如：

离 is a preposition. The prepositional phrase formed by 离 functions as an adverbial in a sentence, indicating the temporal or spatial distance. For example:

1. 我的家离公司很近，可以走着去上班。
2. 我们学校离长城饭店远吗？
3. 今天，离考试还有一个星期。
4. 离上次拜访没有几天，你就不认识我了？

补充生词 Additional New Words

1. 左	zuǒ	left
2. 右	yòu	right
3. 外	wài	outside, outward

练　习
Exercises

一、替换练习。
Substitution drills.

A：你住在哪儿？
B：我住在学校的四号楼。
A：杰克也住四号楼吗？
B：不，杰克住三号楼。

留学生楼	安娜	学校的一号楼
方庄公寓	山口	亚运村公寓
友谊宾馆	史特凡	长城饭店
中国朋友家	谢文	他的爸爸妈妈家

A：你住的学生宿舍一个月付多少房租？
B：一个月 70 美元。
A：谁付？
B：我自己。

留学生楼	240	我爸
公寓	450	学校
饭店	3200	公司
宾馆	4600	老板

二、把下面的词组成句子。
Rearrange the following words into sentences.

1. 我　在　四号　房间　住　215　楼
2. 我　没有　房间　电话　的　里
3. 打　很　方便　我们　不　电话
4. 不　住　外边　学校　喜欢　我们　在

5. 名片　电话　地址　我　和　的　上　有
6. 星期天　我们　老师　去　拜访
7. 学校　错　我们　环境　不　的

三、完成对话。

Complete the following dialogues.

A：你觉得留学生公寓的房租贵吗？
B：________________。

A：________________？
B：我喜欢住在中国朋友家。

A：你为什么不住在学校里边？
B：________________。

A：你觉得住在学校里边方便还是住学校外边方便？
B：________________。

A：你住的公寓环境怎么样？
B：________________。

四、熟读下面的词语，然后用其中的五个词造句。

Read the following words repeatedly, and then choose five of them to make sentences.

里边	外边	上边	下边
左边	右边	前边	后边
里面	外面	上面	下面
左面	右面	前面	后面
以前	以后	以上	以下

五、选择练习四里合适的词语填空。

Fill in the blanks with appropriate words in Exercise 4.

1. 我们学校的环境很好，________是商店，________是饭店，很方便。
2. 对不起，房间________有人睡觉，不能进去。
3. 太太和先生很有意思，在家________先生听太太的，在家________太太听先生的。
4. 开车________要系好安全带。
5. 我们都住在留学生公寓，男学生住在________，女学生住在________。
6. 黑板________写着今天学习的生词。
7. 经理特别客气，把我们送到________才回去。
8. 老板的事太多，吃饭________就开始工作。

六、用"可不"或"可不是"完成对话。

Complete the following dialogues with 可不 or 可不是 .

A：发高烧得去医院检查。

B：____________，____________。

A：住得离学校太远，可不方便。

B：____________，____________。

A：学习汉语有问题应该问老师。

B：____________，____________。

A：你住在长城饭店，房租很贵吧？

B：____________，____________。

七、会话练习。

Situational conversations.

情景 1：你入学时，向留学生部申请住房。

Scene 1: Apply to the Department of International Students for accommodation when you enroll.

情景 2：你在校外向房屋出租者租房。

Scene 2: Rent a room from a landlord outside the university.

八、读拼音，写汉字。

Read the following passage in *pinyin* and then write it out in Chinese characters.

Rìběn liúxuéshēng Shānkǒu, bú zhù xuéxiào, zhù zài Yàyùncūn. Yàyùncūn lí xuéxiào bù yuǎn, huánjìng hěn hǎo, gòuwù, yúlè, dōu hěn fāngbiàn. Dāngrán, Shāngkǒu zuì gāoxìng de shì, tā búyòng fù fángzū. Tā qǐng lǎoshī hé tóngxuémen qù tā jiā wánr. Tóngxuémen shuō, tāmen yǒu kòngr jiù qù bàifǎng Shānkǒu.

24

第二十四课　住在哪儿（二）
Lesson 24　Where Do You Live (II)

课　文
Text

在课外　Zài Kè Wài

珍妮：　嗨，山口，在 这儿 遇上 你 了！
Zhēnnī:　Hēi, Shānkǒu, zài zhèr yùshàng nǐ le!

山口：　真 的，怎么 这么 巧！
Shānkǒu:　Zhēn de, zěnme zhème qiǎo!

杰克：　山口，你 来 买 什么？
Jiékè:　Shānkǒu, nǐ lái mǎi shénme?

山口：　我 来 买 些 家用 电器。
Shānkǒu:　Wǒ lái mǎi xiē jiāyòng diànqì.

珍妮：　亚运村 公寓 没有 电视、冰箱、洗衣机 吗？
Zhēnnī:　Yàyùncūn gōngyù méiyǒu diànshì, bīngxiāng, xǐyījī ma?

山口：　有。我 想 买 一 个 家庭 影院。
Shānkǒu:　Yǒu. Wǒ xiǎng mǎi yí gè jiātíng yǐngyuàn.

珍妮：　现在 网 上 购物 那么 方便，你 干吗 还 去 实体 商店 呢？
Zhēnnī:　Xiànzài wǎng shang gòuwù nàme fāngbiàn, nǐ gānmá hái qù shítǐ shāngdiàn ne?

山口：　网　上　购物，只　能　看　品牌。买　家庭
Shānkǒu:　Wǎng shang gòuwù, zhǐ néng kàn pǐnpái. Mǎi jiātíng
影院，　得　亲眼　看看，体验　体验，才　知道
yǐngyuàn, děi qīnyǎn kànkan, tǐyàn tǐyàn, cái zhīdào
好　不　好。
hǎo bù hǎo.

杰克：　你　就是　想　得　多！
Jiékè:　Nǐ jiùshì xiǎng de duō!

山口：　商店　能　免费　送货　吗？
Shānkǒu:　Shāngdiàn néng miǎnfèi sònghuò ma?

杰克：　恐怕　不行！
Jiékè:　Kǒngpà bùxíng!

珍妮：　我　听说　可以，但　不　能　马上　送。
Zhēnnī:　Wǒ tīngshuō kěyǐ, dàn bù néng mǎshàng sòng.

山口：　只　要　能　送　就　行，等　一两　天，没　关系。
Shānkǒu:　Zhǐ yào néng sòng jiù xíng, děng yì-liǎng tiān, méi guānxi.

珍妮：　嗨！安娜，你　怎么　在　这儿？
Zhēnnī:　hēi! Ānnà, nǐ zěnme zài zhèr?

安娜：　我　就　住　在　这　附近！
Ānnà:　Wǒ jiù zhù zài zhè fùjìn!

山口：　在　哪儿？
Shānkǒu:　Zài nǎr?

安娜：　一　个　四合院。我　住　在　一　个　大娘　的　家　里。
Ānnà:　Yí gè sìhéyuàn. Wǒ zhù zài yí gè dàniáng de jiā li.

杰克：　我们　早　听说　了，老　北京人　都　住
Jiékè:　Wǒmen zǎo tīngshuō le, lǎo Běijīngrén dōu zhù
四合院，是　一　座座　很　有　特色　的　小　平房。
sìhéyuàn, shì yí zuòzuò hěn yǒu tèsè de xiǎo píngfáng.

珍妮：　你　怎么　找到　的？
Zhēnnī:　Nǐ zěnme zhǎodào de?

安娜：　我　在　网　上　发　信息，就　找到　啦。现在
Ānnà:　Wǒ zài wǎng shang fā xìnxī, jiù zhǎodào la. Xiànzài

中国 有 很 多 接待 留学生 的 志愿者 家庭。
Zhōngguó yǒu hěn duō jiēdài liúxuéshēng de zhìyuànzhě jiātíng.

杰克： 你 为 什么 要 住 在 老百姓 家 里？
Jiékè: Nǐ wèi shénme yào zhù zài lǎobǎixìng jiā li?

安娜： 了解 中国 普通 的 人、普通 的 家庭，学习 他们 的 习俗、文化，多 好！
Ānnà: Liǎojiě Zhōngguó pǔtōng de rén, pǔtōng de jiātíng, xuéxí tāmen de xísú, wénhuà, duō hǎo!

山口： 怪不得 你 的 汉语 说 得 这么 好！
Shānkǒu: Guàibude nǐ de Hànyǔ shuō de zhème hǎo!

杰克： 那 你 的 生活 应该 很 有 意思 吧？
Jiékè: Nà nǐ de shēnghuó yīnggāi hěn yǒu yìsi ba?

安娜： 那 当然！ 我们 四合院 住 了 四五 家 人，生活 特别 有 意思。怎么样？ 要 不 要 到 我们 的 四合院 去 看看？
Ānnà: Nà dāngrán! Wǒmen sìhéyuàn zhù le sì-wǔ jiā rén, shēnghuó tèbié yǒu yìsi. Zěnmeyàng? Yào bú yào dào wǒmen de sìhéyuàn qù kànkan?

珍妮： 今天 不行，我们 要 陪 山口 去 商店，改天 一定 去！
Zhēnnī: Jīntiān bùxíng, wǒmen yào péi Shānkǒu qù shāngdiàn, gǎitiān yídìng qù!

安娜： 好，改天 见！
Ānnà: Hǎo, gǎitiān jiàn!

生词 New Words

1. 遇上 yùshàng to meet
2. 巧 qiǎo coincidental

3. 些	xiē	some
4. 家用电器	jiāyòng diànqì	domestic appliances
5. 电视	diànshì	TV
6. 冰箱	bīngxiāng	refrigerator
7. 洗衣机	xǐyījī	washing machine
8. 家庭影院	jiātíng yǐngyuàn	home theatre
9. 网	wǎng	net
10. 干吗	gànmá	why
11. 实体	shítǐ	entity, physical (store)
12. 品牌	pǐnpái	brand
13. 亲眼	qīnyǎn	with one's own eyes
14. 体验	tǐyàn	to experience
15. 免费	miǎnfèi	free (of charge)
16. 恐怕	kǒngpà	I'm afraid
17. 马上	mǎshàng	right away
18. 四合院	sìhéyuàn	quadrangle courtyard
19. 特色	tèsè	feature
20. 平房	píngfáng	bungalow
21. 信息	xìnxī	information
22. 接待	jiēdài	to receive (sb.)
23. 志愿者	zhìyuànzhě	volunteer
24. 老百姓	lǎobǎixìng	ordinary people
25. 普通	pǔtōng	ordinary
26. 习俗	xísú	custom
27. 文化	wénhuà	culture
28. 怪不得	guàibude	no wonder
29. 改天	gǎitiān	another day

注释
Notes

1 “些”，不定量词，它前面的数词只能用“一”，不能用其他数词。例如：

些 (some, a few, a little) is an indefinite measure word, which can be preceded only by the numeral 一 (one). For example:

一些书　　一些笔　　一些香蕉
一些同学　　一些朋友　　一些顾客

“些”还常常用在代词“这、那、哪”的后边。例如：

些 is also often used after such pronouns as 这 (this), 那 (that) and 哪 (which). For example:

这些钱　　这些花　　这些客人
那些货　　那些车　　那些司机
哪些房间　　哪些优点　　哪些问题

2 “恐怕”，副词，表示估计，大体上肯定某事即将发生，但又不是很有把握；有时还表示出某种担心。“恐怕”的后边，常常有助动词“要、能、得”等相呼应。例如：

恐怕, as an adverb, indicates an estimate, more or less affirming that something will happen, but not being very sure. It sometimes expresses a certain degree of anxiety. 恐怕 often corresponds with such an auxiliary verb as 要, 能, and 得 that comes after it. For example:

1. 明天我恐怕不能来，你不要等我了。
2. 这事儿，你恐怕得找经理。
3. 他恐怕已经走了二十多天了。
4. 你要是再误事，恐怕老板要开除你了！

“恐怕”有时候还表达一种委婉的口气。说话人其实已经有了自己的想法，但用估计、商量的语气说出来。句尾常常有“吧”字。例如：

恐怕 sometimes expresses a mild tone. The speaker has actually formed his own opinion, but expresses it in a tone of estimation or consultation. Such sentences often end with the character 吧. For example:

1. 这恐怕不行吧。
2. 你这样做，恐怕不好吧！
3. 这个价格恐怕太高了吧！
4. 他们俩在这儿见面，恐怕不是巧遇吧！

3 “马上”，副词，表示事情很快就要发生。例如：

马上, an adverb, indicates that something will happen very soon. For example:

1. 出租车马上就来。
2. 你应该马上付房租。
3. 我马上就去见经理。
4. 你马上打电话叫她来！

“马上”还表示两件事接连发生，后一件事情紧接着前一件事情。例如：

马上 also indicates that two events happen consecutively, with the second one happening right after the first. For example:

1. 你先去吧，我马上就来。
2. 我下班后马上回家。
3. 他听了我的话，好像马上想起了什么。
4. 他刚走，看样子不会马上回来。

4 “怪不得”，副词，表示明白了原因，对某种情况就不再觉得奇怪。例如：

怪不得 is an adverb which means that one will not feel strange about something after knowing the reason. For example:

1. 他考得不太好，怪不得不高兴。
2. 他住在学校里，怪不得来得这么早。
3. 他今天过生日，怪不得收到了这么多礼物。

补充生词
Additional New Word

1. 收费 shōu fèi to charge (a fee)

练　习
Exercises

一、替换练习。
Substitution drills.

网上购物那么方便，你干吗还去实体商店？

在食堂吃饭	自己做饭
坐地铁	坐公共汽车
在家看电影	去电影院
用微信	打电话

A：今天能送货吗？
B：恐怕不行。

经理今天回来	回不来
你明天和我们一起去	不能去
今天下午你有空儿	没有空儿
公司能给我付房租	不行

二、把下面的词组成句子。
Rearrange the following words into sentences.

1. 就　她　附近　在　这　住
2. 这　巧　真是　太　了
3. 我们　洗衣机　用　衣服　洗
4. 现在　都　一些　电器　家家　有　家用
5. 他们　货　不能　送　马上　恐怕

三、完成对话。

Complete the following dialogues.

A：________________________。
B：怪不得他今天没来。

A：他喜欢和中国人聊天儿。
B：怪不得__________________。

A：________________________。
B：怪不得他今天迟到了。

A：他的汽车坏了。
B：怪不得__________________。

四、从下面选择适当的量词填空。

Fill in the blanks with the appropriate measure words.

件　些　笔　辆　瓶　次　点儿

1. 我要赚____钱去旅行。
2. 这____生意，他赚了不少钱。
3. 你这是第几____迟到了？
4. 出门不带____现金不方便。
5. 我买了一____新车。
6. 她只吃了一____东西就睡了。
7. 巧了，这____人我都认识。
8. 做什么事都只能一____一____地做。
9. 这____问题，我不能立即回答。
10. 他去看朋友的时候，带了一____葡萄酒。

五、用“恐怕”和括号里的词完成下面的句子。

Complete the following sentences with 恐怕 and the words in the brackets.

1. 这么晚了，______________。（出租车）
2. 他病得很厉害，______________。（住医院）
3. 我几天都没接到她的电话了，______________。（不在北京）
4. 现在常常堵车，______________。（早一点儿）
5. 你要是再误事，______________。（开除）
6. 我现在很忙，______________。（马上）

六、会话练习。

Situational conversations.

情景 1：在商店买东西，同商家谈送货上门的事。

Scene 1: You are shopping at a store. Discuss with the assistant about home delivery.

情景 2：打电话给接待留学生的中国家庭，询问相关信息。

Scene 2: Call the Chinese families that host international students and ask for relevant information.

七、阅读下面的一段话，然后用拼音把这段话写出来。

Read the following passage, and then write it in *pinyin*.

珍妮和杰克陪山口去买家庭影院。山口想去实体商店买，因为可以亲眼看看，体验体验，还能免费送货。他们在商店附近遇上了安娜。安娜住在一个四合院里。那里住了四五家人，生活很有意思。安娜请他们有空儿去四合院看看。

25

第二十五课　今天怎么样（一）

Lesson 25　What's the Weather Like Today（Ⅰ）

课　文

Text

在课上　Zài Kè Shang

杰克：　安娜，今天 怎么样？
Jiékè:　Ānnà, jīntiān zěnmeyàng?

安娜：　今天 我的 身体 很 好！
Ānnà:　Jīntiān wǒ de shēntǐ hěn hǎo!

杰克：　我 知道你的 病 早就好了，身体 很 好。
Jiékè:　Wǒ zhīdao nǐ de bìng zǎo jiù hǎo le, shēntǐ hěn hǎo.

安娜：　那你问 什么？
Ānnà:　Nà nǐ wèn shénme?

杰克：　我 问 今天 天气 怎么样？
Jiékè:　Wǒ wèn jīntiān tiānqì zěnmeyàng?

安娜：　嗯…… 看 样子 不错。
Ānnà:　Ǹg…　Kàn yàngzi búcuò.

杰克：　最 高 气温 多少 度？
Jiékè:　Zuì gāo qìwēn duōshao dù?

安娜：　我 不 知道。
Ānnà:　Wǒ bù zhīdào.

杰克：　你没 听 天气 预报？
Jiékè:　Nǐ méi tīng tiānqì yùbào?

安娜：　　我 哪里 听 得 懂？
Ānnà:　　Wǒ nǎli　tīng de dǒng?

杰克：　　我们　去 问问 老师 吧。
Jiékè:　　Wǒmen qù wènwen lǎoshī ba.

安娜：　　王　老师，我们　怎么 听 天气 预报？
Ānnà:　　Wáng lǎoshī, wǒmen zěnme tīng tiānqì yùbào?

王　老师：啊，这 很 容易。我们 这儿　正好　有 今天 的
Wáng lǎoshī: Ā,　zhè hěn róngyì. Wǒmen zhèr zhènghǎo yǒu jīntiān de
　　天气 预报 录音，你们 听听。
　　tiānqì yùbào lùyīn, nǐmen tīngting.

安娜：　　那 太 好 了！
Ānnà:　　Nà tài hǎo le!

听众　　朋友，你们 好！现在　播送 24
Tīngzhòng péngyou, nǐmen hǎo! Xiànzài bōsòng 24
小时　城市　天气 预报：北京，今天　晚上
xiǎoshí chéngshì tiānqì yùbào: Běijīng, jīntiān wǎnshang
多云　转 阴，有 小雨，最 低 气温 20℃；
duōyún zhuǎn yīn, yǒu xiǎoyǔ, zuì dī qìwēn 20℃;
明天　白天，多云　转　晴，风力 2～3 级，
míngtiān báitiān, duōyún zhuǎn qíng, fēnglì 2～3 jí,
最 高 气温 28℃。
zuì gāo qìwēn 28℃.

王　老师：你们　听懂　了 吗？
Wáng lǎoshī: Nǐmen tīngdǒng le ma?

杰克：　　听懂　了 一点儿。
Jiékè:　　Tīngdǒng le　yìdiǎnr.

安娜：　　我 一点儿 也 没　听懂。
Ānnà:　　Wǒ yìdiǎnr yě méi tīngdǒng.

王　老师：别 着急，多 听 几 遍 就 会　听懂　的。
Wáng lǎoshī: Bié zháojí,　duō tīng jǐ biàn jiù huì tīngdǒng de.

生词 New Words

1. 身体	shēntǐ	body, health
2. 天气	tiānqì	weather
3. 看样子	kàn yàngzi	to look like, to look as if
4. 气温	qìwēn	air temperature
5. 预报	yùbào	to forecast
6. 哪里	nǎli	*used in rhetorical questions to express negation*
7. 懂	dǒng	to understand, to know
8. 正好	zhènghǎo	just in time, just right
9. 录音	lùyīn	recording
10. 听众	tīngzhòng	audience, listeners
11. 播送	bōsòng	to broadcast, to transmit
12. 城市	chéngshì	city
13. 多云	duōyún	cloudy
14. 阴	yīn	overcast
15. 雨	yǔ	rain
16. 白天	báitiān	daytime, day
17. 晴	qíng	clear, fine
18. 风力	fēnglì	wind force, wind power
19. 级	jí	level, rank
20. 高	gāo	high
21. 着急	zháojí	worried, anxious
22. 遍	biàn	(*a measure word*) time

注释
Notes

1 “看样子”，意思是看情形，看趋势。表示一种估计。例如：

看样子 has the meaning of judging by the circumstances or tendency. It expresses an estimate. For example:

1. 看样子他今天不会来了。
2. 看样子今天要下雨。
3. 看样子，这事不那么容易做好。
4. 风停了，看样子今天是个晴天。

2 “哪里”，代词，表处所，如“你从哪里来？”；也可以用在反问句中表示否定，这时没有处所的意思；用来单独答话，表示对对方称赞的否定，是一种客气的说法。例如：

哪里, a pronoun, indicates a place, as in 你从哪里来?(Where are you from?) It can also be used in a rhetorical question to indicate negation. In this case it doesn't indicate a place. When it is used as a reply by itself, it is a polite response to compliments or thanks. For example:

1. 你从哪里来，我早听说了。
2. 他哪里是美国人，他是法国人。
3. 他哪里病了，他是不想上课。
4. 我哪里是什么大经理？
5. A：小姐，这事太麻烦你了！
   B：哪里，哪里，快别客气。

3 “正好”，副词，表示两件事或两种情况的巧合。例如：

正好 is an adverb which indicates that two things or two circumstances just coincide with each other. For example:

1. 现在天气很好，正好去旅行。
2. 这些钱正好买一张飞机票。
3. 这几天我正好休息，可以陪你去玩儿。
4. 她开始工作的时候，正好二十岁。

"正好"，有时可以做句子的谓语、补语，有时还可以单独成句。这时的"正好"是个实词，意思相当于"正合适"。例如：

正好 can function as the predicate or complement of a sentence. Sometimes it can be used by itself. In that case, 正好 is a notional word, with its meaning being 正合适 (just right). For example:

1. 你来得正好，经理刚从外边回来。
2. 这间办公室不大不小，正好。
3. A：多少钱？
   B：十二元五角。
   A：给你。
   B：您的钱正好。

补充生词 Additional New Words

1. 雪	xuě	snow
2. 零下	língxià	below zero
3. 风	fēng	wind

练习 Exercises

一、替换练习。

Substitution drills.

A：他爸爸的病怎么样？
B：看样子病快好了。

身体	还不错
工作	挣了很多钱
生意	不是很好
旅行	很顺利

A：他没有听老师讲课？
B：他哪里听得懂。

去打工	有时间
去做生意	会做
买车	有那么多钱
叫你一声	记得我这个老同学

A：你能陪我去商店吗？
B：行，我正好休息。

书店	想买几本书
医院	要去看大夫
留学生办公室	要去交学费
听力教室	想听天气预报录音

二、把下面的词组成句子。

Rearrange the following words into sentences.

1. 你　怎么样　身体　的
2. 今天　多少　气温　最高　白天　度
3. 我　大　预报　不　天气　相信
4. 他　工作　着急　找　不
5. 请　说　一遍　你　再

三、完成对话。

Complete the following dialogues.

A：你常常听天气预报吗？
B：不，＿＿＿＿＿＿＿＿＿＿＿＿。

A：你旅行的时候，喜欢什么样的天气？
B：＿＿＿＿＿＿＿＿＿＿＿＿＿＿。

A：你旅行的时候，最怕遇上什么样的天气？
B：＿＿＿＿＿＿＿＿＿＿＿＿＿＿。

A：下雨天，你在家都做些什么？

B：______________________________。

A：______________________________？

B：别着急，你只是感冒了，不是什么大病。

四、模仿例句说话。

Make sentences following the example.

例句：看样子，今天天气不错。

1. 他俩的友谊
2. 这辆汽车
3. 出租车
4. 着急
5. 容易做

五、下面是天气预报的常用词，先熟读，然后听一听、说一说今天的天气预报。

Read repeatedly the following words often used in weather forecasts. Then listen to and talk about today's weather forecast.

白天——晚上（夜间）　最高——最低　阴——晴

气温　度　零下　云　雨　雪　风

风力　级　转

六、会话练习。

Situational conversation.

情景：朋友见面，开始总是先问好，然后谈今天天气怎么样。听，两个朋友的谈话就这样开始了……

Scene: When friends meet, they first greet each other and then start talking about the weather. Here are two friends start talking in this way...

七、读拼音，写汉字。

Read the following passage in *pinyin* and then write it out in Chinese characters.

Jīntiān de kǒuyǔ kè, tóngxuémen xuéxí zěnme tīng tiānqì yùbào. Tiānqì yùbào shuō, wǎnshang yǒu yǔ, zuì dī wēndù língxià qī dù. Míngtiān báitiān duōyún zhuǎn qíng, fēnglì bú dà, zuì gāo wēndù shí'èr dù. Míngtiān tiānqì búcuò, Jiékè, Zhēnnī hé Shānkǒu zhǔnbèi chūqù wánr.

26

第二十六课　今天怎么样（二）

Lesson 26　What's the Weather Like Today (II)

课　文

Text

在课外　Zài Kè Wài

珍妮：　杰克，你看，好像要下雨了！
Zhēnnī:　Jiékè, nǐ kàn, hǎoxiàng yào xià yǔ le!

杰克：　天气预报不是说今天没有雨吗？
Jiékè:　Tiānqì yùbào bú shì shuō jīntiān méiyǒu yǔ ma?

山口：　珍妮还说今天天气好呢！
Shānkǒu:　Zhēnnī hái shuō jīntiān tiānqì hǎo ne!

珍妮：　天气预报是这么说的嘛！怎么说变天就变天了呢？
Zhēnnī:　Tiānqì yùbào shì zhème shuō de ma! Zěnme shuō biàn tiān jiù biàntiān le ne?

杰克：　老师说过，北京天气的特点是夏天炎热多雨，冬天寒冷干燥，春天干旱多风。
Jiékè:　Lǎoshī shuōguo, Běijīng tiānqì de tèdiǎn shì xiàtiān yánrè duō yǔ, dōngtiān hánlěng gānzào, chūntiān gānhàn duō fēng.

山口：　北京的秋天最好，没风少雨，不冷
Shānkǒu:　Běijīng de qiūtiān zuì hǎo, méi fēng shǎo yǔ, bù lěng

不 热。
bú rè.

珍妮： 我 忘了 老师 的 话 了，现在 正 是 多雨 的 季节，出门 的 时候 就 应该 带上 雨衣。
Zhēnnī: Wǒ wàngle lǎoshī de huà le, xiànzài zhèng shì duō yǔ de jìjié, chūmén de shíhou jiù yīnggāi dàishàng yǔyī.

山口： 我们 骑着 自行车，现在 怎么 回 学校 呢？
Shānkǒu: Wǒmen qízhe zìxíngchē, xiànzài zěnme huí xuéxiào ne?

杰克： 我 有 办法，跟 我 来！
Jiékè: Wǒ yǒu bànfǎ, gēn wǒ lái!

杰克： 小姐，外边 下 雨 了，我们 没有 带 雨具，可以 借 给 我们 吗？
Jiékè: Xiǎojie, wàibian xià yǔ le, wǒmen méiyǒu dài yǔjù, kěyǐ jiè gěi wǒmen ma?

小姐： 当然 可以。要 雨衣 还是 雨伞？
Xiǎojie: Dāngrán kěyǐ. Yào yǔyī háishì yǔsǎn?

杰克： 我们 骑 自行车，要 雨衣。
Jiékè: Wǒmen qí zìxíngchē, yào yǔyī.

小姐： 好 的。
Xiǎojie: Hǎo de.

杰克： 我们 必须 什么 时候 还 回来？
Jiékè: Wǒmen bìxū shénme shíhou huán huílái?

小姐： 你们 来 商店 的 时候，顺便 带来 就 可以 了。
Xiǎojie: Nǐmen lái shāngdiàn de shíhou, shùnbiàn dàilái jiù kěyǐ le.

杰克： 必须 送到 你们 商店 来 吗？
Jiékè: Bìxū sòngdào nǐmen shāngdiàn lái ma?

小姐： 啊，不。本 市 几十 家 商场 都 有 这 项 服务，你们 可以 送到 离 你们 最 近 的 一
Xiǎojie: Ā, bù. Běn shì jǐshí jiā shāngchǎng dōu yǒu zhè xiàng fúwù, nǐmen kěyǐ sòngdào lí nǐmen zuì jìn de yì

家　商店。
jiā shāngdiàn.

杰克：　谢谢！
Jiékè:　Xièxie!

珍妮：　杰克，你　好像　跟　那　位　小姐　很　熟？
Zhēnnī:　Jiékè,　nǐ hǎoxiàng gēn nà wèi xiǎojie hěn shóu?

杰克：　不。我们　不　认识。
Jiékè:　Bù. Wǒmen bú rènshi.

珍妮：　那　你　怎么　知道　她　肯　借　给　你　雨具？
Zhēnnī:　Nà nǐ zěnme zhīdào tā kěn jiè gěi nǐ yǔjù?

杰克：　中国　朋友　告诉　我，在　商店　可以　借到　雨具。
Jiékè:　Zhōngguó péngyou gàosu wǒ,　zài shāngdiàn kěyǐ jièdào yǔjù.

山口：　商店　不怕借的人不　还　吗？
Shānkǒu:　shāngdiàn bú pà jiè de rén bù huán ma?

杰克：　文明伞，　大家　用。　相信　大家都　讲　文明　嘛！
Jiékè:　Wénmíngsǎn, dàjiā yòng. Xiāngxìn dàjiā dōu jiǎng wénmíng ma!

生　词
New Words

1. 变　biàn　to change, to transform
2. 特点　tèdiǎn　characteristic
3. 夏天　xiàtiān　summer
4. 炎热　yánrè　hot
5. 冬天　dōngtiān　winter
6. 寒冷　hánlěng　cold

7. 干燥	gānzào	dry
8. 春天	chūntiān	spring
9. 干旱	gānhàn	arid
10. 秋天	qiūtiān	autumn
11. 冷	lěng	cold
12. 热	rè	hot
13. 季节	jìjié	season
14. 出门	chūmén	to go out, to leave home, to go on a journey
15. 雨衣	yǔyī	raincoat
16. 骑	qí	to ride, to sit on the back of
17. 自行车	zìxíngchē	bicycle
18. 办法	bànfǎ	method, way, means
19. 跟	gēn	to follow; with
20. 雨具	yǔjù	rain gear
21. 借	jiè	to borrow, to lend
22. 雨伞	yǔsǎn	umbrella
23. 必须	bìxū	must, to have to
24. 还	huán	to give back, to return, to go back
25. 顺便	shùnbiàn	by the way
26. 本市	běn shì	this city
27. 商场	shāngchǎng	shop, department store
28. 项	xiàng	*a measure word for itemized things*
29. 位	wèi	*a measure word for people*
30. 熟	shóu	familiar, well-acquainted, ripe, cooked
31. 肯	kěn	to be willing to, to agree, to consent
32. 文明	wénmíng	civilization; civilized
33. 讲	jiǎng	to speak, to tell, to pay attention to

注释 Notes

1 “不是……吗”，是一个反问句的格式，强调肯定，有时带有惊讶或不满的语气。例如：

不是……吗 is used in rhetorical questions to emphasize certainty and sometimes implies surprise or dissatisfaction. For example:

1. 你不是回家了吗？怎么还在这儿？
2. 我不是告诉你了吗？为什么你不知道？
3. 我不是把书给你了吗？
4. 这不是我买的水果吗？

2 趋向补语：一些动词后边常用“来、去、上、下、上来、下去、起来、出去、进来”等词做补语，表示动作的方向。例如：

Complement of direction: Some verbs take such words as 来 (to come), 去 (to go), 上(up), 下 (down), 上来 (to come up), 下去 (to go down), 起来 (to arise), 出去 (to go out), and 进来 (to come in), etc. as the complements, indicating the direction of movement. For example:

1. 谁呀？请进来！
2. 我看见汽车已经开出去了。
3. 请你站起来说吧！
4. 这天真的下起雨来了。

3 “跟”，介词，介绍出动作的另一个施动者。当一个动作有两个参与者时，“跟”字前面的施动者处于主导地位，两个施动者的前后顺序不能颠倒。例如：

跟 is a preposition to introduce the other agent of an action. When an action has two participants, the one mentioned before 跟 is in the dominant position, and they cannot be transposed. For example:

1. 我跟她吵？是她跟我吵！
2. 我不跟他说话，我们没有什么好说的。
3. 不是我不想跟她交朋友，是她不想跟我交朋友。

"跟"还可以介绍出动作的对象。例如：

跟 can also introduce the recipient of an action. For example:

1. 你快跟大家说说，她的病怎么样了。
2. 你别走，我跟你说点儿事。
3. 我现在没有钱，我可以跟朋友借。

补充生词 Additional New Words

1. 吵（架）	chǎo (jià)	to quarrel, to have a row
2. 潮湿	cháoshī	moist, damp
3. 凉快	liángkuai	cool, nice and cool
4. 暖和	nuǎnhuo	warm, nice and warm

练习 Exercises

一、替换练习。

Substitution drills.

A：我们必须什么时候来？

B：你们最好在八点以前来。

出差	下个星期三	出差
离开宾馆	十二点	离开
去机场	飞机起飞	到机场
完成工作	老板来检查	完成

A：你好像跟那位小姐认识？
B：我们见过两次面。

杰克	很熟悉	我们是朋友
什么人	吵架了	有的人真没礼貌
我	借过 500 元	我下个星期一定还
老板	说了些什么	我想让他知道一些事

二、把下面的词组成句子。

Rearrange the following words into sentences.

1. 她　电话　的　变　号码　了
2. 北京　干燥　冬天　春天　的　很　和
3. 很　喜欢　多　骑　人　自行车
4. 你　办法　什么　好　有　吗
5. 你　大家　肯　都　帮助

三、完成对话。

Complete the following dialogues.

A：北京哪个季节多风？
B：____________________。

A：你喜欢骑自行车旅行吗？
B：____________________。

A：____________________？
B：没有，我们去买一把雨伞吧！

A：你不怕我借了你的钱不还吗？
B：____________________。

A：要是你去请他，他会来吗？
B：不，____________________。

四、模仿例句说话。

Make sentences following the example.

例句：刚才还是好天气，怎么说变就变了呢？

1. 吵架
2. 不来
3. 收费
4. 卖完

五、选词填空。

Fill in the blanks with the proper words provided.

顺便　　随便　　方便

1. 你们想喝什么就喝什么，请别客气，我的家很____。
2. 你去银行能____为我兑换点儿钱吗？
3. 这儿环境很好。买东西，娱乐，都很____。
4. 你别看他很有钱，其实他吃东西不讲究，很____。
5. 我们这儿，上班可以坐公交车和地铁，很____。
6. 出门旅行带很多现金不____。
7. 我来北京出差，____拜访了多年没见的一位老朋友。
8. 请别误会，我只是____问问。

特别　　　特点

1. 这个酒吧很有____，葡萄酒____好。
2. 北京冬天____干燥。
3. 不能随便交朋友，____是女孩子。
4. 北京人说话很有____，你说是吗？
5. 她的____是跟什么人都熟。

6. 他有很多中国朋友，所以，他的听和说都____好。
7. 快餐的____就是快！
8. 你都说了，我没什么____要说的。

六、填空。

Fill in the following blanks.

一年有____个季节。它们是____、____、____、____。北京的春天从____月到____月，夏天从____月到____月，秋天从____月到____月，冬天从____月到____月。北京的冬天最____，最____，很少下____。春天很____，不过常常____。夏天多____，白天特别____。秋天最好，多____天，很少刮____下____。我开始不____北京的天气，现在慢慢____了。

七、会话练习。

Situational conversations.

情景1：介绍你们国家或你们家乡的天气。

Scene 1: Talk about the weather of your country or hometown.

情景2：杰克他们去商场借的雨伞为什么叫"文明伞"？商场为什么开展出借"文明伞"的服务？

Scene 2: Talk about the "Civilized Umbrellas" lent out by the store Jack and Jenny went to. Why do the stores provide this kind of service?

八、读拼音，写汉字。

Read the following passage in *pinyin*, and then write it out in Chinese characters.

Jiékè, Zhēnnī hé Shānkǒu yìqǐ chūqù wánr. Hǎohāor de qíngtiān shuō biàn jiù biàn, qíng zhuǎn yīn, yíhuìr, xiàqǐ yǔ lái le. Tāmen dōu qí zìxíngchē, yòu méi dài yǔjù, zěnme bàn? Háishi Jiékè yǒu bànfǎ. Tā dài dàjiā dào yì jiā shāngchǎng, jièle sān jiàn yǔyī. Zhēnnī hé Shānkǒu dōu hěn qíguài, Jiékè zěnme néng zài shāngchǎng jièdào yǔyī ne? Yuánlái shāngchǎng gěi gùkè zhǔnbèile shéi dōu kěyǐ jiè de wénmíngsǎn.

27

第二十七课　逛北京（一）

Lesson 27　Going Sightseeing in Beijing（Ⅰ）

课　文

Text

在课上　Zài Kè Shang

王　老师：同学们，　你们 来 北京 多 久 了？
Wáng lǎoshī: Tóngxuémen, nǐmen lái Běijīng duō jiǔ le?

杰克：　　我 来 北京 快 一 年 了。
Jiékè: 　　Wǒ lái Běijīng kuài yì nián le。

珍妮：　　我 来了 还 不 到 半 年。
Zhēnnī: 　　Wǒ láile hái bú dào bàn nián.

王　老师：你们　逛过　北京 了 吗？
Wáng lǎoshī: Nǐmen guàngguo Běijīng le ma?

杰克：　　我 和 珍妮 常 去。
Jiékè: 　　Wǒ hé Zhēnnī cháng qù.

王　老师：山口　呢？
Wáng lǎoshī: Shānkǒu ne?

山口：　　我 坐 出租车　逛过　几 次。
Shānkǒu: 　　Wǒ zuò chūzūchē guàngguo jǐ cì.

杰克：　　那 还 叫 逛？ 骑 自行车 去 才 叫 逛　呢！
Jiékè: 　　Nà hái jiào guàng? Qí zìxíngchē qù cái jiào guàng ne!

山口：　　我 不 认 路，骑 自行车 出去，怕 回 不 了 家。
Shānkǒu: 　　Wǒ bú rèn lù, 　qí zìxíngchē chūqù, pà huí bu liǎo jiā.

珍妮：　找 个 人带路啊！
Zhēnnī:　Zhǎo gè rén dàilù a!

山口：　找 谁？
Shānkǒu:　Zhǎo shéi?

杰克：　我 啊！我 是个 老 北京 了。
Jiékè:　Wǒ a! Wǒ shì gè lǎo Běijīng le.

王 老师：杰克，你 说 你是老 北京？
Wáng lǎoshī: Jiékè, nǐ shuō nǐ shì lǎo Běijīng?

杰克：　不 好意思，开开 玩笑。
Jiékè:　Bù hǎo yìsi, kāikai wánxiào.

王 老师：你到底熟悉不熟悉 北京 呢？
Wáng lǎoshī: Nǐ dàodǐ shúxi bù shúxi Běijīng ne?

杰克：　说 不 上 熟悉，不过骑自行车，丢不了。
Jiékè:　Shuō bu shàng shúxi, búguò qí zìxíngchē, diū bu liǎo.

山口：　你有 什么 办法？
Shānkǒu:　Nǐ yǒu shénme bànfǎ?

杰克：　这 很 简单。北京 的大街、胡同、马路，都是笔直笔直的，不是 南北 方向，就是东西 方向。
Jiékè:　Zhè hěn jiǎndān. Běijīng de dàjiē, hútòng, mǎlù, dōu shì bǐzhí bǐzhí de, bú shì nánběi fāngxiàng, jiùshì dōngxī fāngxiàng.

珍妮：　只要 记住我们 学校 在 什么 地方，就 丢不了。
Zhēnnī:　Zhǐyào jìzhù wǒmen xuéxiào zài shénme dìfang, jiù diū bu liǎo.

山口：　那也 不行，我 分不 清 东西 南北。
Shānkǒu:　Nà yě bùxíng, wǒ fēn bu qīng dōngxī nánběi.

杰克：　这 也 有 办法，你 只要 记住 向 左 拐，往 右 拐……
Jiékè:　Zhè yě yǒu bànfǎ, nǐ zhǐyào jìzhù xiàng zuǒ guǎi, wǎng yòu guǎi…

山口：　不行，不行。拐 来 拐 去，还不拐 糊涂了？
Shānkǒu:　Bùxíng, bùxíng. Guǎi lái guǎi qù, hái bù guǎi hútu le?

珍妮：　山口，你还是花钱坐出租车吧。坐出租车不会糊涂，哈，哈，哈……
Zhēnnī:　Shānkǒu, nǐ háishi huā qián zuò chūzūchē ba. Zuò chūzūchē bú huì hútu, hā, hā, hā…

生词 New Words

1. 逛	guàng	to stroll, to ramble, to roam, to go sightseeing
2. 久	jiǔ	long, for a long time
3. 带路	dàilù	to lead the way, to act as a guide
4. 玩笑	wánxiào	joke, jest
5. 到底	dàodǐ	finally, on earth, after all
6. 熟悉	shúxi	to know sth. (or sb.) well, to be familiar with
7. 丢	diū	to lose, to mislay, to put aside
8. 大街	dàjiē	main street
9. 胡同	hútòng	lane, alley
10. 笔直	bǐzhí	perfectly straight
11. 南	nán	south
12. 北	běi	north
13. 方向	fāngxiàng	direction, orientation
14. 东	dōng	east
15. 西	xī	west
16. 地方	dìfang	place, locality
17. 分	fēn	to divide, to distinguish
18. 清（楚）	qīng (chu)	clear, distinct
19. 向	xiàng	direction; to turn towards
20. 拐	guǎi	to turn
21. 往	wǎng	in the direction of, towards
22. 糊涂	hútu	muddled, confused

注释
Notes

1 “到底”，副词，用在疑问句中，追究事情的真相。句中或句尾常有疑问词，或全句是一个选择式问句。例如：

到底 is an adverb used in an interrogative sentence to look into the actual state of affairs. Such a sentence normally contains a question word in the middle or at the end of it, or the whole sentence is an alternative question. For example:

1. 你快说，到底怎么了？
2. 你们说啊，到底是谁把雨伞拿走了？
3. 这件事，他到底清楚不清楚啊？
4. 你到底去不去？大家都在等你呢！

2 “胡同”，就是城市里比较狭窄的小街道，一般称作“巷”，与宽阔的大街相对而言，所谓“大街小巷”。不过，以北京为中心的几个北方城市把小巷称为“胡同”。尤其是在北京，“胡同”好像是北京城市的独特景观。人们说起胡同，就自然会想到北京；说起北京，就自然会想到它的胡同。北京的胡同旅游，是近几年来北京非常吸引外国人的特色旅游。

Hutong is a narrow lane in a city. It is normally referred to as 巷 (lane or alley), contrasting with wide streets, as in 大街小巷 (wide streets and small lanes). It is only in a few northern cities with Beijing as the center that lanes are referred to as *hutong*. *Hutong* seems to be a unique scenery in the city of Beijing. Whenever *hutong* is mentioned, people will think of Beijing or vice versa. Beijing *hutong* tour is a distinctive touring item in Beijing that is developed in recent years and is most attractive to foreign friends.

3 “不是……就是……”，这种“不是 A 就是 B”的格式中，前后两项中必有一项是事实。例如：

In this pattern of “不是A就是B”, one of the two must be factual. For example:

1. 不是你去，就是我去。
2. 这天，不是刮风就是下雨。
3. 今天吃饭，不是你付钱就是我付钱。

4 “向”，介词，由“向”组成的介词词组，表示动作的方向或趋向。这时同“往”的意义和用法差不多。例如：

向 is a preposition used to form a prepositional phrase denoting the direction or trend of an action. In such cases, 向 is similar to 往 in meaning and usage. For example:

1. 师傅，请向右拐。
2. 他向胡同口走去。
3. 向前走三个房间，就是王老师的办公室。
4. 向左拐有一个银行。

“向”还可以介绍出行为和动作的对象。例如：

向 is also used to introduce the recipient of an action or behavior. For example:

1. 我向大家介绍一下，这是我们公司的总裁万先生。
2. 这事儿，你向她说清楚了吗？
3. 我要向他学习。
4. 你如果遇到什么麻烦，就向大家说吧，大家会帮助你的。

5 “往”，介词，与表方位或地点的词语组成介词词组，表示行为或动作的方向，可在句子中做状语。例如：

往 is a preposition used to form a prepositional phrase with words denoting direction or location. The prepositional phrase thus formed indicates the direction of an action or a movement, functioning as an adverbial in the sentence. For example:

1. 你往前走，就能看见我们学校了。
2. 往南走不远就是368路车站。
3. 你往后看，谁来了？
4. 师傅，请再往前开一点儿！

“往”组成的介词词组，也可以做补语或定语，跟在它后边的多是表地点的词语，而不是方位词。例如：

The prepositional phrase with 往 can also function as a complement or an attribute. The words that follow it are often words denoting locality rather than nouns of locality. For example:

1. 请问，这是开往上海的火车吗？

2. 这些是送往长城饭店的鲜花。
3. 飞往纽约（Niǔyuē New York）的航班已经起飞了。

补充生词 Additional New Words

1. 北海公园　Běihǎi Gōngyuán　Beihai Park
2. 颐和园　Yíhé Yuán　Summer Palace
3. 天安门　Tiān' ān Mén　Tian'anmen
4. 西单　Xīdān　Xidan

练　习 Exercises

一、替换练习。
Substitution drills.

A：你来北京多久了？
B：我来北京<u>三个月</u>了。
A：你去过<u>天安门</u>吗？
B：我去过一次。

半年	王府井
一年	长城
一个学期	颐和园
一年零两个月	上海

A：你去哪儿？
B：逛<u>商店</u>。
A：你一个人去吗？
B：不，我跟<u>山口</u>一起去。

西单	安娜
王府井	杰克
北海公园	珍妮
颐和园	一个中国朋友

A：你到底认识不认识钱先生？
B：认识，不过不熟悉。

喜欢	这种手表	不想买
想	去上海	没有钱
会	开车	开得不太好
能	完成工作	不是现在

二、把下面的词组成句子。

Rearrange the following words into sentences.

1. 这　个　玩笑　是　只　开
2. 我　喜欢　这　玩笑　不　个
3. 你　什么　了　丢
4. 我　自行车　了　丢　的
5. 今天　真　糊涂　我
6. 你们　在　地方　学校　什么
7. 这　问题　很　个　简单

三、完成对话。

Complete the following dialogues.

A：你能分清东西南北吗？
B：________________。

A：你们公司在什么地方？
B：________________。

A：________________？
B：你跟我来，我带你去。

A：你知道他为什么没来上班吗？
B：不很清楚，他好像________________。

四、模仿例句说话。

Make sentences following the example.

例句：北京的大街，不是南北方向，就是东西方向。

1. 星期天　　宿舍　　教室
2. 太太出门　　开车　　叫出租车
3. 我的手表坏了　　快　　慢
4. 杰克去天安门　　走路　　骑自行车
5. 他有点儿糊涂　　拿错书　　忘了上课时间

五、为下列各句填上合适的介词。

Fill in the blanks with the proper prepositions.

从　　往　　向

1. 不能上课要____老师请假。
2. 你____哪儿走？
3. 上班时，经理总是先____大家问好。
4. ____前走，就对了；____后退，就错了。
5. 不要总是觉得自己对，要多听听别人怎么说，要____别人学习。
6. 他记得____去年夏天开始，他不怕说汉语了。
7. ____北京人问路，他告诉你____南拐，____前走到十字路口，再____北拐就到了；____上海人问路，他告诉你____左拐，____前走到十字路口，再____右拐就到了，很有意思。
8. 我们三个人都是____南方来的。

六、下面是北京市示意图，请你按下面的要求说说骑自行车怎样去目的地。

Below is a sketch map of Beijing. Please explain how you can get to the required destinations by bike.

说话时用上下面的词。

Use the following words in your talk.

向　往　拐　一直　左　右　前　后　东　西

南　北　从　到

例如：从经贸大学骑自行车去天安门，应该怎么走？

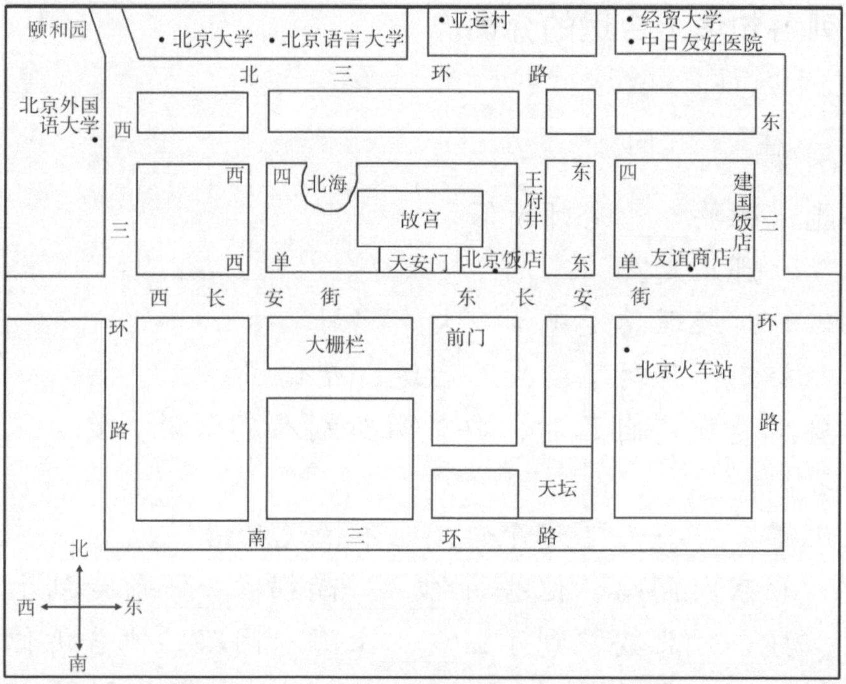

七、朗读下面的拼音，试一试能不能用汉字把这段话写出来。

Read aloud the following tongue twisters and antithetical couplets in *pinyin*, and try to write them out in Chinese characters.

绕口令和对联

Tongue twisters and antithetical couplets in *pinyin*

Māma qí mǎ, mǎ màn māma, mà mǎ.

（Mum is riding a horse. The horse is slow, and Mum scolds the horse.）

Shūshu zhòng shù, shù shǎo, shūshu shǔ shù.

(Uncle is planting trees. Some trees are missing, and uncle counts the trees.)

Shí bú shì sì, sì bú shì shí.

(Ten is not four and four is not ten.)

Shísì shì shísì, sìshí shì sìshí.

(Fourteen is fourteen, and forty is forty.)

Sìshí jiā sì shì sìshísì.

(Forty plus four is forty-four.)

28

第二十八课 逛北京（二）

Lesson 28 Going Sightseeing in Beijing (II)

课 文

Text

在课外 Zài Kè Wài

山口： 杰克，我们 去 哪儿？
Shānkǒu: Jiékè, wǒmen qù nǎr?

杰克： 先 去 王府井， 然后 去 前门 大栅栏 和 西单。
Jiékè: Xiān qù Wángfǔjǐng, ránhòu qù Qiánmén Dàshílánr hé Xīdān.

山口： 为 什么 去 那儿？
Shānkǒu: Wèi shénme qù nàr?

珍妮： 这 是 北京 最 繁华 的 三 条 商业 街。
Zhēnnī: Zhè shì Běijīng zuì fánhuá de sān tiáo shāngyè jiē.

山口： 好，走 吧，我 跟着 你们。
Shānkǒu: Hǎo, zǒu ba, wǒ gēnzhe nǐmen.

杰克： 前面 就 是 王府井 了，我们 把 车 存 在 这儿 吧，走 的 时候 好 取。
Jiékè: Qiánmian jiù shì Wángfǔjǐng le, wǒmen bǎ chē cún zài zhèr ba, zǒu de shíhou hǎo qǔ.

山口：嗬，好热闹！门脸儿挨着门脸儿，商店真多啊！
Shānkǒu: Hē, hǎo rènao! Ménliǎnr āizhe ménliǎnr, shāngdiàn zhēn duō a!

珍妮：听，那儿在吆喝什么？"停一停，看一看，买一送一啰！""换季大甩卖啰！"
Zhēnnī: Tīng, nàr zài yāohe shénme? "Tíng yi tíng, kàn yi kàn, mǎi yī sòng yī luo!" "Huànjì dà shuǎimài luo!"

杰克：听不大懂，好像是叫人停下来买他的东西。
Jiékè: Tīng bu dà dǒng, hǎoxiàng shì jiào rén tíng xiàlái mǎi tā de dōngxi.

山口：走，去看看！
Shānkǒu: Zǒu, qù kànkan!

杰克：我们到西单北大街了！
Jiékè: Wǒmen dào Xīdān Běidàjiē le!

山口：这儿跟大栅栏不太一样，倒是跟王府井差不多。
Shānkǒu: Zhèr gēn Dàshílánr bú tài yíyàng, dàoshì gēn Wángfǔjǐng chàbuduō.

珍妮：大栅栏是条传统商业街，街道窄，门面古色古香。
Zhēnnī: Dàshílánr shì tiáo chuántǒng shāngyè jiē, jiēdào zhǎi, ménmiàn gǔsè-gǔxiāng.

杰克：王府井和西单，是现代化商业街，高楼大厦，好气派！
Jiékè: Wángfǔjǐng hé Xīdān, shì xiàndàihuà shāngyè jiē, gāo lóu dàshà, hǎo qìpài!

珍妮：世界各地的东西，在这些商场差不多都能买到。
Zhēnnī: Shìjiè gè dì de dōngxi, zài zhèxiē shāngchǎng chàbuduō dōu néng mǎidào.

山口：　真 的？都 是 进口 货 吗？
Shānkǒu:　Zhēn de? Dōu shì jìnkǒu huò ma?

杰克：　不！进口 货， 中国 货，什么 都 有 人 卖，什么 都 有 人 买。
Jiékè:　Bù! Jìnkǒu huò, Zhōngguó huò, shénme dōu yǒu rén mài, shénme dōu yǒu rén mǎi.

珍妮：　中国 真 是 人 多，商店 多，东西 多，卖 什么 都 有 人 买，生意 好 做，钱 好 赚。
Zhēnnī:　Zhōngguó zhēn shì rén duō, shāngdiàn duō, dōngxi duō, mài shénme dōu yǒu rén mǎi, shēngyi hǎo zuò, qián hǎo zhuàn.

山口：　听 你 这 口气，你 好像 已经 在 中国 市场 上 赚了 大钱 了！
Shānkǒu:　Tīng nǐ zhè kǒuqì, nǐ hǎoxiàng yǐjīng zài Zhōngguó shìchǎng shang zhuànle dàqián le!

杰克：　哈，恭喜 发财！
Jiékè:　Hā, gōngxǐ fācái!

珍妮：　同喜！同喜！
Zhēnnī:　Tóngxǐ! Tóngxǐ!

生词 New Words

1. 然后　ránhòu　then, afterwards
2. 繁华　fánhuá　flourishing, bustling, busy
3. 条　tiáo　*a measure word for long, narrow or thin things*
4. 商业　shāngyè　commerce
5. 街（道）　jiē (dào)　street
6. 存　cún　to leave with, to deposit
7. 取　qǔ　to take, to get, to fetch

8. 嗬	hē	ah, oh
9. 热闹	rènao	lively, bustling with noise and excitement
10. 门脸儿	ménliǎnr	shop front
11. 挨	āi	to be next to
12. 吆喝	yāohe	to cry out, to call, to shout
13. 换季	huànjì	to change garments proper for the season
14. 甩卖	shuǎimài	to have a markdown sale
15. 倒是	dàoshì	*indicating concession, contrast, or sth. unexpected*
16. 差不多	chàbuduō	about the same, similar, almost
17. 传统	chuántǒng	tradition
18. 窄	zhǎi	narrow
19. 门面	ménmiàn	shop front, appearance
20. 古色古香	gǔsè-gǔxiāng	antique
21. 大厦	dàshà	large building, mansion
22. 气派	qìpài	imposing manner, dignified air
23. 世界	shìjiè	world
24. 各地	gè dì	various places
25. 进口	jìnkǒu	to import
26. 口气	kǒuqì	tone, note, manner of speaking
27. 市场	shìchǎng	market
28. 恭喜	gōngxǐ	to congratulate
29. 发财	fācái	to get rich, to make a fortune

专 名 Proper Nouns

1. 前门	Qiánmén	Qianmen
2. 大栅栏	Dàshílánr	Dashilanr

注释
Notes

1 “跟”，介词，引出表示比较的对象。“跟”后面常有“相同”“一样”“差不多”“相反”等词语相呼应。例如：

跟 is a preposition introducing the object of comparison. 跟 often echoes with such words as 相同 (identical), 一样 (the same), 差不多 (about the same), or 相反 (the opposite). For example:

1. 我跟他一样，也是美国人。
2. 我跟他不一样，见了人他不爱说话，我爱说话。
3. 这辆车跟那辆车的价钱差不多。
4. “门脸儿”跟“门面”的意思差不多。

2 “倒是”，副词，表示不以为然，或强调与事实相反，或表示让步。例如：

倒是 is an adverb expressing disapproval, stressing that it is contrary to the fact, or expressing a concession. For example:

1. 我倒是没什么，就怕她不高兴。
2. 他倒是说得容易，让他去试试看！
3. 东西倒是好，就是太贵了。
4. 我倒是想帮助你，只是手头没有钱。
5. 该说的你不说，不该说的你倒是说个没完。
6. 我先生倒是天天回来，只是回来就要睡觉，难得同他说几句话。

“倒是”还可以表示催促、深究。例如：

倒是 is also used to express urging, or delving into a matter. For example:

1. 你倒是去不去？
2. 你倒是快一点儿啊，汽车要开了！
3. 你倒是去找她啊，有什么不好意思的！
4. 到底怎么回事，你倒是说呀！

3 “差不多”，表示近似的意思，说明事件或情况跟某种程度、数量、性状等相差无几。有时是一种强调，有时是一种估计。例如：

差不多 means “similar”, indicating that an event or a situation is not much different from a certain degree, quantity, or property. Sometimes it expresses an emphasis, and sometimes an estimate. For example:

1. 我的钱差不多都花完了。
2. 现在常常堵车，坐车跟走路差不多。
3. 这三条街差不多一样繁华。
4. 他做生意差不多快三十年了。

4 “恭喜发财”，这是中国很流行的一句客套话。在春节，人们见面，互相一拱手，就说“恭喜发财！”对对方表示新年的良好祝福。生意场上，人们见面，也常常用这句话表示问候和祝贺，甚至询问对方在哪儿做生意，也这样问：“您在哪儿发财呀？”

恭喜发财 (congratulations and may you make a fortune) is a polite formula which is very popular in China. During the Spring Festival, when people meet, they would make a cupped-hand salute to each other and say 恭喜发财, which is a New Year benediction on the other party. On business occasions, when people meet, they often use it as a greeting or benediction. Even when they ask the other party where they are doing business, they would say: “您在哪儿发财呀？” (Where are you making your fortune?)

补充生词 Additional New Words

1. 国产	guóchǎn	made in one’s country, home-made
2. 出口	chūkǒu	to export
3. 内销	nèixiāo	to sell in domestic market
4. 化妆品	huàzhuāngpǐn	cosmetics

练习
Exercises

一、替换练习。
Substitution drills.

A：你觉得他说的汉语怎么样？

B：他说的汉语跟你差不多。

这家商店	别的商店
进口货	国产货
出口商品	内销商品
中国化妆品	外国化妆品

A：听你的口气，你好像考得很好？

B：你说得没错，这次考试我得了 A。

发财了	我刚赚了五万元
得了便宜	商店今天买一送一
找到了工作	我明天就上班
遇到了麻烦	我的自行车丢了

二、把下面的词组成句子。
Rearrange the following words into sentences.

1. 我们　地方　存　找个　车　吧
2. 要　存　收费　自行车　吗
3. 街　这些　很　商业　都　繁华
4. 很　进口　人　多　只　商品　相信
5. 你　应该　说话　用　不　口气　这种

三、写出下列词语的反义词。
Give the antonyms of the following words.

大——	多——	买——
好——	进——	借——
对——	快——	远——
存——	冷——	贵——
难——	糊涂——	潮湿——
进口——	内销——	优点——

四、完成对话。

Complete the following dialogues.

A：________________________？
B：取车的时候交费。

A：那个人在吆喝什么？
B：________________________。

A：你看这辆新车怎么样？
B：________________________！

A：你倒底愿不愿意借钱给我？
B：________________________。

A：恭喜发财！
B：________________________，________________________！

五、模仿例句说话。

Make sentences following the example.

例句：这儿的环境倒是不错。

1. 很热闹
2. 一路顺利
3. 天气很好
4. 方向没错
5. 价格便宜

例句：这儿跟王府井差不多。

1. 北京的房租
2. 我的身高
3. 今天的天气
4. 这儿的菜
5. 北京好玩儿的地方

六、会话练习。

Situational conversations.

情景1：几个朋友骑自行车逛北京的商业街，边走，边看，边说。

Scene 1: Several friends are roaming around the shopping streets of Beijing by bike.They look and talk on their way.

情景2：有人在吆喝“买一送一”，你相信这是好事，你的朋友不相信。你想出很多理由，想说服你的朋友。

Scene 2: Someone is shouting in a shop: “Buy one and get one free.” You believe it is a good thing, but your friend doesn’t. Try to convince your friend.

七、朗读下面的拼音，试一试能不能用汉字把这些对联写出来。

Read aloud the following *pinyin*, and try to write them out in Chinese characters.

Chéng zhāo wǔzhōu guìkè kè liú kè qù jiē wéi guìkè.

(Sincerely we entertain distinguished guests from the five continents. Staying or leaving, they are all distinguished guests.)

Xiào yíng sìhǎi jiābīn bīn lái bīn wǎng jìn shì jiābīn.

(Smilingly we welcome honored guests from the four seas. Coming or going, they are all honored guests.)

Wèi jǐ máng wèi rén máng máng li tōu xián hē hú xiāng chá xiāoxiao hàn.

(You are busy for yourself, and you are busy for the others. To snatch a little leisure from a busy life, please come and drink a pot of fragrant tea and dispel your sweat.)

Láo xīn kǔ láo lì kǔ kǔ zhōng qiú lè chī wǎn liángfěnr qīngqing xīn.

(It’s hard to work with one’s brain, and it’s hard to work with one’s brain. To find relief from your hardship, please come and have a bowl of bean jelly and clear up your mind.)

英译课文

English Translation of the Texts

Lesson 1 Hello

1. A: Hello.
   B: Hello.

2. A: How do you do, Miss?
   B: How do you do?

3. A: Hi, Anna.
   B: Hi, Jack.

4. A: Good morning, Anna.
   B: Good morning, Jack.

5. A: Hi, Anna.
   B: Hi, Jack.
   A: How are you?
   B: Very well, thank you. And you?
   A: I'm fine, too.

Lesson 2 Who Is He

1. A: How do you do? My name is Xie Wen.
   B: I'm Anna. How do you do?
   A: Very nice to meet you.
   B: Very nice to meet you, too.

2. A: Are you the manager?
   B: Oh, no. I'm the secretary. He is the manager.

A: Oh, I'm sorry.

B: That's all right.

3. A: Hello, Manager. I'm Anna.

B: Hello, Miss Anna. Who is she?

A: This is Julia.

C: Julia Levy. I am from the United States.

B: Hello, very glad to meet you.

C: Very glad to meet you, too.

4. A: Good morning, Manager.

B: Good morning, Anna.

A: My name is Julia.

B: Oh, yes. Hello, Mrs. Julia.

A: Miss, Miss Julia Levy.

B: Oh, I'm sorry, Miss Levy.

A: That's all right.

Lesson 3 My Friends

1. A: Hi, Anna. Do you know Yamaguchi?

B: Who is Yamaguchi?

A: My Japanese friend.

B: I'm sorry. I don't know her.

2. A: Xie Wen, who is that?

B: Yamaguchi.

A: Is she an international student?

B: Yes. We are classmates.

A: Are you friends?

B: Yes, we are good friends.

3. A: Hi, Yamaguchi.

C: Hi, Xie Wen.

A: Yamaguchi, let me introduce you to each other. This is my friend, Anna.

C: Is she your girlfriend?

A: Anna, what would you say?

B: No, I'm not his girlfriend.

Lesson 4 How to Address a Person

1. A: What's your family name?

B: It's Wan.

A: What's your given name?

B: Wenjie. (My name is) Wan Wenjie.

2. A: Come in, please.

B: Are you Mr. Gao?

A: Yes, I'm Gao Ya'an. What's your name?

B: My surname is Wan. My full name is Wan Wenjie.

A: Oh, Mr. Wan, sit down, please.

B: Thanks.

3. A: May I ask your family name?

B: My family name is Wan, Wan Wenjie.

A: Oh, Mr. Wan. Very pleased to meet you.

B: Very pleased to meet you, too.

Lesson 5 Making Telephone Calls

1. A: Hello.

B: Hello. Is Mrs. Xie in?

A: You've got the wrong number.

B: I'm sorry.

2. A: Hello. This is Aiyou Company.

B: Hello. Is Mr. Gao Ya'an in?

A: He is not in. Can I help you?

B: Oh, please ask him to call me back.

A: Your phone number is...

B: 68370641.

A: OK. Bye-bye.

3. A: Hello, is that 68370641?

B: That's right. This is Wan Wenjie.

A: This is Gao Ya'an.

B: I phoned you and you were not in.

A: Is there anything I can do for you?

B: Do you have Mrs. Xie's telephone number?

A: Yes. It's 64960057.

B: Good. Thanks.

Lesson 6 Booking a Room

1. A: Hello. This is the service desk of Beijing Hotel.

B: I would like to book a room.

A: A suite?

B: No. A standard (double) room.

A: When will you be arriving?

B: Tomorrow.

A: What is your surname, please?

B: My surname is Wang.

A: We will be expecting your arrival.

2. A: Miss, I would like to have a room, please.

B: Do you have any reservation?

A: Yes, I made a reservation yesterday by phone.

B: What's your surname, please?

A: My surname is Wang.

B: Just a moment. Room 3702. Will that do?

A: That's fine. Thank you.

B: You're welcome.

Lesson 7 Changing Money

1. A: Miss, we would like to change some money.
   B: Cash or traveler's checks?
   A: Cash.
   C: Mine is a traveler's check.
   B: How much do you want to change?
   A: What's the exchange rate for today?
   B: 100 US dollars to 689.80 *yuan*.
   A: OK. I'll exchange 500 US dollars. How about you?
   C: I won't exchange any.

2. A: Miss, I exchanged 500 US dollars just now.
   B: Is there anything wrong?
   A: Today's exchange rate is 100 US dollars to 689.80 *yuan*. Is that right?
   B: That's right.
   A: Then 500 US dollars should be exchanged for 3,459 *yuan*?
   B: It's 3,449 *yuan*, Mister, not 3,459.
   A: Oh, I got it wrong. I'm sorry.
   B: That's OK.

Lesson 8 Taxi

1. A: Taxi!
   B: Mister, get on, please. Where are you going?
   A: To Beijing Hotel.
   B: Take your seat.
   A: Please pull up when you get to the Friendship Store.
   B: OK.

2. B: Are you taking a tour?
   A: No, I come here to do business.
   B: Have you just arrived in Beijing?
   A: Yes, how do you know?

B: I'm a taxi driver.

A: Have we got to the Friendship Store?

B: No, We are stuck in a traffic jam.

A: Oh.

3. B: Here is Beijing Hotel, Mister.

A: How much is it?

B: 48 *yuan*.

A: Here is fifty *yuan*.

B: Here is your 2 *yuan* change.

A: Please give me a receipt.

B: OK.

A: Thank you.

B: Goodbye.

Lesson 9 He Has Not Turned up for Work

1. A: Xiao Wang, get the car ready for me, please.

B: When do you need it?

A: In half an hour.

B: OK.

2. A: Hello, is Master Zhang there?

B: No, he's not in.

A: Where is he?

B: He has not turned up for work.

A: Oh, thanks.

3. A: Hello. This is the general service desk of the hotel.

B: Hello. This is Aiyou Company. We would like to have a car.

A: When do you want it?

B: 9:45.

A: That is in fifteen minutes, right?

B: Yes. Is that OK?

A: No problem.

B: Thank you.

4. A: Manager, the car has been arranged.

B: Thank you.

A: It will be at the gate of the hotel in fifteen minutes.

B: Is Master Zhang driving?

A: No, Master Zhang is absent today. It is a car from the hotel.

B: All right. I see.

Lesson 10 It Is Her Birthday Today

1. A: Oh, what beautiful flowers!

B: These are for you.

A: For me? Xiao Wang, you...

B: I bought them for you.

A: But I didn't ask you to buy flowers.

(The phone rang, and B answered the phone.)

B: Hello, Mrs. Qian. Yes, he's in. Hold on a second. Manager, you are wanted on the phone.

2. A: Hello, darling, what's the matter?

B: What time is it now?

A: Six o'clock sharp.

B: Aren't you coming home yet?

A: Oh, I'm sorry. I've got an appointment this evening.

B: Have you forgotten what day it is today?

A: Friday, October 30.

B: Who asked you that?

3. A: Xiao Wang, my wife just called me and she seemed to be very angry.

B: Why?

A: She asked me what day today is.

B: What did you say?

A: I said that it was Friday, October 30.

B: And your wife hung up?

A: Yes. Did I give the wrong date?

B: No, you didn't.

A: Why was she angry then?

B: It is your wife's birthday today, my great manager.

A: Oh, my God. Thank you for the flowers you bought. And please cancel my appointment tonight.

Lesson 11 What Do You Want to Do（I）

(In class)

Professor Wang: Hello, everybody. Do you all know each other?

Jack: Let me introduce myself first.

Yamaguchi: No need for introduction. I know that you are Jack from the United States.

Jack: And I know that you are Yamaguchi from Japan.

Jenny: We all know each other.

Yamaguchi: I also know that Jenny has come to China to learn Chinese.

Jenny: Do you know why I am studying Chinese?

Yamaguchi: That goes without saying. You study Chinese so that you can do business in China in the future.

Jenny: Right, but not completely.

Jack: What do you mean?

Jenny: Jack, let me ask you why you are studying Chinese.

Jack: I like to make friends.

Jenny: What about you, Yamaguchi?

Yamaguchi: Me? I like to have fun. How can I travel in China if I don't know Chinese?

Professor Wang: You all said that you knew Jenny, didn't you?

Jack: Yes, we all know her.

Professor Wang: Do you know her well?

Yamaguchi: No, not yet.

Jenny:	No, we don't know each other well enough.
Yamaguchi:	Jack and I don't quite understand what Jenny said just now.
Professor Wang:	Jenny, isn't it for doing business that you are studying Chinese?
Jenny:	To be an attendant is also doing business.
Jack:	You don't want to be an attendant, do you?
Jenny:	No.
Yamaguchi:	What about a secretary?
Jenny:	No.
Jack:	What do you want to do then?

Lesson 12 What Do You Want to Do (II)

(After class)

Attendant:	Welcome, welcome. Please come in.
Manager Liu:	How are you, Professor Wang?
Professor Wang:	You are...
Manager Liu:	You don't recognize me, Professor Wang? I'm Liu Liang, your former student.
Professor Wang:	Oh, it's you, Liu Liang. Are you here to have fun too?
Manager Liu:	No, I'm the manager of this bar.
Professor Wang:	Really? I remember you have worked only for three years, and now you are already a manager?
Manager Liu:	You forgot that I studied business administration, professor?
Professor Wang:	No, I didn't. You worked hard and studied well.
Manager Liu:	Professor Wang, what would you like to drink? Please make yourselves at home.
Professor Wang:	Anything, tea, Coca-Cola, or orange juice.
Jack:	Beer, please.
Manager Liu:	Fine. Attendant!
Jenny:	Mr. Liu, is it true that you have become a manager only after three years' working?
Manager Liu:	Yes, it's true.
Jack:	Jenny, do you also want to be a manager of a bar?

Jenny: Why can't I? I want to be a boss or even a CEO.
Jack: Of course it's all right, but ...
Jenny: But what?
Jack: You have to come here to be an attendant first.
Jenny: Why?
Jack: One should learn how to walk before learning how to run.
Yamaguchi: Jenny can run before learning how to walk, ha ....

Lesson 13 Can You Speak Chinese（I）

(In class)
Professor Wang: Everybody, who can speak Chinese?
Jack: I can, but I don't speak it well.
Jenny: I have just started studying Chinese, and I can just speak a little.
Professor Wang: I didn't mean that, for I know all of you can speak a little Chinese.
Jenny: What did you mean then, professor?
Professor Wang: Let me give you a test first. How do you ask for help?
Jenny: All right, let me try.
Jenny: Hey, old chap, where is Peking University?
Jack: Hey, whose name is Hey? Don't you know how to address people?
Jenny: Oh, I'm sorry. Grandpa, could you tell me where Peking University is?
Professor Wang: That's right. The old man will be glad to tell you now.
Jack: Yes, one should be polite when asking for help.
Professor Wang: Let's try again.

Yamaguchi: Driver, go to the Great Wall Hotel.
Taxi driver: I'm not going.
Yamaguchi: Hey, why are you going away?
Jack: Of course he would go away. Who let you call him "Driver"?
Yamaguchi: What should I call him then?

Jack:	You should call him *shifu* (Master). "*Shifu*, I'm going to the Great Wall Hotel."
Yamaguchi:	That's right. You are so polite and how could the driver be annoyed?
Professor Wang:	Now do you understand what I mean by that question?
Jenny:	Yes, I do.

Lesson 14 Can You Speak Chinese (II)

(After class)

Jenny:	Jack, the Chinese lesson yesterday was very interesting indeed.
Jack:	You are right. It is really not easy to speak Chinese well.
Jenny:	Let's have some more practice together.
Jack:	Fine. I'll play the shop assistant, and you the customer. How about that?
Jenny:	Good. Let's begin.

Jack:	Miss, welcome to shop here.
Jenny:	Welcome me to buy things? Can't I just come to have a look round and don't buy anything?
Jack:	Oh, welcome. Do as you please.
Jenny:	Look, you make inapproprite remarks and the customer was angry.

Jack:	OK, let's try again. Miss, what do you want?
Jenny:	What did you say? Have I come to ask for things?
Jack:	I didn't mean that, please don't misunderstand me.
Jenny:	Did I misunderstand you, or you didn't say the right thing?
Jack:	Oh, I'm sorry.

Jack:	Look, I got it wrong again.
Jenny:	You shouldn't say: "What do you want?"
Jack:	What should I say then?
Jenny:	You should say: "Miss, what do you intend to buy?"

Jack: No, that's not right. "I don't want to buy anything. Can't I just have a look round?"

Jenny: Eh. The customer would also get angry if you said that.

Jack: What should I say then?

Jenny: Oh, it's too difficult. I don't know what to say either.

Lesson 15 Do You Know How to Make Purchases（I）

(In class)

Professor Wang: Hello, everybody, do you know how to make purchases?

Jenny: Yes, I'll cash on delivery.

Jack: That simple?

Professor Wang: You can have a try and see whether it is that simple.

Jack: Hey, how much is one *jin* of these apples?

Jenny: Jack, don't buy here.

Jack: Why? You don't know how to bargain?

Jenny: It's not that I don't know how, but we can't do it here.

Jack: Why?

Jenny: This apple seller is my friend's father.

Jack: All right.

Jenny: How much is one *jin* of these apples?

Peddler: Twelve *yuan* for three *jin*.

Jenny: Three *jin* for ten *yuan*, OK?

Peddler: Ten *yuan* for two and a half *jin*.

Jenny: What? That is still four *yuan* a *jin*.

Jack: You are really capable of cheating.

Jenny: Ten *yuan* for three *jin*. If you don't agree, we'll go.

Peddler: OK, OK. Ten *yuan* for three *jin*.

Jenny: How was that? I bargain it down by two *yuan*.

Jack: You're really good at shopping.

Lesson 16 Do You Know How to Make Purchases (II)

(After class)

Jenny:	Jack, do you like reading advertisements?
Jack:	No, I don't, but I have to.
Jenny:	Why?
Jack:	How can I buy things without reading ads?
Jenny:	Do you know how to make purchases after reading ads?
Jack:	Of course. If you don't believe, we can have a try.
Jenny:	Then..., let's go and buy a watermelon.
Jack:	Let's go.

Jenny:	Jack, have a look at the words written on this small blackboard.
Jack:	One *jin* for 1.50 *yuan*. Authentic American Watermelon 118, with the shortcoming of being too sweet.
Jenny:	American watermelon sold in China. Have you ever tasted it?
Jack:	No, not yet.
Jenny:	What do you think? Shall we buy some?
Jack:	Yes, the watermelon is sweet and I like it.

Jack:	How much is a *jin* of these melons?
Peddler:	One and a half *yuan* for one *jin*.
Jack:	That's too expensive. Could you make it a bit cheaper?
Peddler:	No, I can't. This is authentic American Watermelon 118.
Jack:	What is written on the small blackboard is not deceptive, is it?
Peddler:	How can it be?
Jack:	Good. Pick one for me.
Peddler:	OK.
Jack:	How much is it?
Peddler:	It's 11 *jin* and a half. That's 17.25 *yuan*. Let's make it 17 *yuan*.

Jack: Please cut a small cone piece (and let's have a look).
Peddler: OK.
Jack: How come that the melon is not sweet at all?
Peddler: It is clearly written here. Its shortcoming is too sweet. Then its merit is not sweet.
Jack: Oh, this ad of yours ...

Lesson 17 We Can't Do Without It（I）

(In class)

Professor Wang: I want to ask you a question. What can't you do without?
Jack: Jenny couldn't do without her mum.
Yamaguchi: Jenny couldn't live without her Barbie dolls.
Professor Wang: My question is what you can't do without now?
Jenny: Mobile phone! We can't live without it!
Jack: Right. None of us can live without it.
Professor Wang: One day people suddenly find that everyone, from young people to senior people, has a mobile phone.
Yamaguchi: It is a good thing. It proves that mobile phones are popular in China.
Professor Wang: Yes, you are right. What else have you found?
Jack: Many people lower their heads and absorb themselves in phones all the time even when they take a class, walk on the road, or ride in a car.
Yamaguchi: I heard that a university student missed the bus stop and jumped out of the bus from the window.
Jenny: How dangerous it is!
Professor Wang: Yes. You can talk about how to safely and efficiently use your mobile phone after class.

Lesson 18 We Can't Do Without It（II）

(After class)

Jenny: Jack! Yamaguchi! Let's finish the homework together!

Yamaguchi: OK. I'll ask you first. Can you do without mobile phones?

Jack: Of course not! I need to date with my girlfriend every day. I can't do without my phone.

Jenny: I need to call my mum every day. I cannot do without it either.

Jack: It is easy to connect to the Internet, so people can't do without mobile phones.

Yamaguchi: Yes! I like ordering takeout using it!

Jenny: I know. You always sleep late and choose takeout.

Yamaguchi: Yes, it is very convenient!

Jack: I also order takeout if I want to eat a hamburger.

Jenny: Mobile phones can almost help us do anything including ordering takeout.

Yamaguchi: Yes. I haven't been to the bank or shop for a long time. We buy things online with our mobile phones.

Jack: You can also take a taxi, book air tickets, and buy gifts for your girlfriend with a mobile phone.

Jenny: We become lazier and lazier.

Jack: No! We learn to enjoy life!

Yamaguchi: Enjoy modern life!

Jack: Now WeChat helps us make a lot of friends and keep abreast of the news.

Jenny: But Professor Wang reminded us to use mobile phones safely.

Yamaguchi: Jack, don't play with your mobile phone when crossing the road any more!

Jack: Have I ever done that?

Lesson 19 What's the Matter with Her (I)

(In class)

Professor Wang: Good morning, everybody.

Students: Good morning, Professor.

Professor Wang: Is everybody here?

Jenny:	Anna and Jack aren't here.
Professor Wang:	Anything wrong with them?
Jenny:	Anna is sick, and Jack has accompanied her to the hospital.
Professor Wang:	What's wrong with her?
Jenny:	Perhaps she's caught a cold. She said that she was not feeling well.
Professor Wang:	Was she running a fever? Has she had her temperature taken?
Jenny:	Yes, 38.5 degrees centigrade.
Professor Wang:	Oh, that's quite high. Did she have a cough?
Jenny:	No, and her throat wasn't sore either. But she was always feeling thirsty.
Professor Wang:	She should drink plenty of water.
Jenny:	That won't do, for she had diarrhea.
Professor Wang:	In that case, she should drink even more water.
Jenny:	Won't that aggravate her diarrhea?
Professor Wang:	Oh, no, it won't.
Yamaguchi:	I think that maybe she didn't catch a cold. Perhaps she ate something bad.
Professor Wang:	Now let's begin our class. We'll go and see her after class.

Lesson 20 What's the Matter with Her（II）

(After class)

Qian Fucheng:	Mister, are you on a tour?
Jack:	Yes, what about you?
Qian Fucheng:	I am on a business trip, being engaged in trade.
Jack:	Doing business? Why don't you travel by air?
Qian Fucheng:	To save some money by bearing hardships.
Jack:	But traveling by train is too slow. Businessmen pay most attention to time.
Qian Fucheng:	That's right. Time is money.
Jack:	But...
Qian Fucheng:	It doesn't matter. It's off day today.
Jack:	That's right. Nobody would be at work today.

Qian Fucheng:	How come that your friend is sleeping all the way?
Jack:	She is not feeling well.
Qian Fucheng:	Why is she just sleeping without taking some medicine?
Jack:	She was fine when she got on the train and she started getting sick last night, and we want to buy some medicine when we get off the train.
Qian Fucheng:	Oh, please wait a minute and I'll go and get a doctor.

Qian Fucheng:	The doctor is here.
Doctor:	What's wrong with you, Miss?
Anna:	I have a terrible headache.
Doctor:	Oh, you are running a fever. Let me take your temperature.

Doctor:	Give me the thermometer, please. Forty degrees centigrade. That's too high. Let me have a look at your throat.
Jack:	Anything wrong?
Doctor:	Her throat has got inflamed.
Jack:	Does she need an injection? She is afraid of that.
Doctor:	Let her take some antipyretics first, once every four hours, two tablets each time.
Anna:	Doctor, is it serious?
Doctor:	Go and have a thorough check-up in the hospital after you get off the train.
Anna:	Oh, don't let me be hospitalized!

Lesson 21 Whose Fault Is It (I)

(In class)

Jack:	Hello, Professor.
Professor Wang:	Hello. Why are you late again today?
Jack:	But I am not late! Look, my watch says it's 7:50. Actually I've come early.
Jenny:	7:50? It's already 8:15. You're fifteen minutes late.
Jack:	How could that be? Your watch must be wrong.

Professor Wang:	All right. Sit down and take out your book please.
Jack:	Oh, too bad.
Jenny:	You have brought the wrong book again, haven't you?
Jack:	Isn't this the listening comprehension class by Professor Zhang? How come this is Professor Wang's class?
Jenny:	This is Professor Wang's oral class.
Jack:	I felt odd when I entered the classroom just now. What day is it today?
Jenny:	It's Tuesday today.
Jack:	Tuesday? Look, today is Monday according to my watch.
Jenny:	I was wondering why you didn't come to class yesterday. Now I see. You thought yesterday was Sunday.
Jack:	But I didn't take a rest. I was working to earn some money.

Professor Wang:	What were you two talking about?
Jenny:	Jack thought it was Monday today, and he has only brought the book for listening comprehension.
Jack:	Professor, I'm not to blame. It's my watch that is wrong. I guarantee that it won't be wrong again tomorrow.
Yamaguchi:	Who's to blame then if you are late again for class tomorrow?
Jack:	Yes, who should be blamed then? Myself? Oh, no...

Lesson 22 Whose Fault Is It（II）

(After class)

Jack:	(Excuse me,) Miss, at what time is Express No. 14 from Shanghai arriving?
Miss:	Express No. 14 should be arriving at one minute past nine. It's only half past seven now. It's too early.
Jack:	What? Only half past seven?
Miss:	Yes. Look! The clock on the tall building says it's half past seven now.
Jack:	No. I've just set my watch. It's now half past eight. The

clock on that tall building must be slow.

Miss: How could that be? It's your watch that is fast.

Jack: Is it? This damn watch made me get up very early, and now I have to wait for more than an hour.

Miss: Have you come to meet somebody?

Jack: Yes, to meet a friend of mine from Shanghai.

Miss: Is this your friend's first visit to Beijing?

Jack: No, he often comes to Beijing by train on business. It's my first time to come to the railway station.

Miss: Oh, in that case, it's your friend who should have come to meet you.

Jack: Why?

Miss: Because he wouldn't have said that the clock on that tall building was wrong.

Jack: Hi, Steven, I'm here!

Steven: Hi, Jack, nice to meet you.

Jack: Was it a nice trip?

Steven: Everything's fine.

Jack: Everything is always fine with you, but I often run into troubles.

Steven: What was wrong?

Jack: This damn watch of mine always holds things up.

Steven: What's wrong with your watch?

Jack: It was slow during the last few days so that I was late for class several times. Today it is fast and makes me wait for you here for more than one hour.

Steven: Ha... You will be fired if you are an employee in my company.

Lesson 23 Where Do You Live (I)

(In class)

Professor Wang: Jack, where do you live?

Jack:	In Building No. 4 of our university.
Professor Wang:	What about you, Jenny?
Jenny:	Also in Building No. 4.
Professor Wang:	In which room then?
Jenny:	On the third floor, Room 347. And Jack lives on the second floor, Room 215.
Professor Wang:	How many people are there in your room?
Jack:	Two.
Professor Wang:	Is there a phone in your room?
Jenny:	Yes. There is only one telephone. Sometimes when my rommate uses it, I can't.
Jack:	Right.
Yamaguchi:	Well, it is not very convenient.
Jack:	Yamaguchi is lucky for she lives outside the campus.

Professor Wang:	Where do you live, Yamaguchi?
Yamaguchi:	Near the Asian Games Village, not far from the university.
Professor Wang:	Why don't you stay in the university?
Jenny:	It is very expensive to live outside the university.
Yamaguchi:	The firm my husband works for has rented an apartment for us, and we don't have to pay the rent.
Jenny:	How's the environment?
Yamaguchi:	Very good. It's very convenient for shopping or for recreation.
Jenny:	Oh, that's superb.
Yamaguchi:	You are all welcome to visit my home. This is my husband's card, with the address and telephone number on it.
Jenny:	Thank you. We would really like to go to visit you when we have time.

Lesson 24 Where Do You Live（II）

(After class)

Jenny:	Hi, Yamaguchi. Fancy meeting you here!
Yamaguchi:	Indeed, it's a nice surprise.

Jack: Yamaguchi, what do you intend to buy?

Yamaguchi: I have come for some household electric appliances.

Jenny: Isn't the apartment at the Asian Games Village equipped with a TV, a fridge and a washing machine?

Yamaguchi: Yes. But I would like to have a home theatre.

Jenny: Since it is very convenient to shop online, why do you still go to physical stores?

Yamaguchi: You can only choose the brand when shopping online. If you want to buy a home theatre, you need to see it for yourself before knowing whether it is good or not.

Jack: You always think too much.

Yamaguchi: Do physical stores provide free delivery service?

Jack: I'm afraid not.

Jenny: I heard that they would help you deliver goods, but not immediately.

Yamaguchi: I can wait for one or two days. It is OK as long as the stores provide the service.

Jenny: Hi, Anna! Why are you here?

Anna: I live nearby.

Yamaguchi: Where?

Anna: In a quadrangle courtyard owned by an aunt.

Jack: We've long known that old natives of Beijing live in quadrangle courtyards, which are very distinctive bungalows.

Jenny: How did you find it?

Anna: Through an online post. Many Chinese families are willing to host foreign students.

Jack: Why would you live in an ordinary Chinese family?

Anna: It is wonderful to know ordinary Chinese people and families as well as learn their customs and culture.

Yamaguchi: No wonder your spoken Chinese is so great!

Jack: Your life must be very interesting.

Anna: Of course! There are four to five families in the quadrangle courtyard. Life there is very interesting! How about going to see it?

Jenny: We cannot go today because we need to go to the store with Yamaguchi. We will go there another day!

Anna: OK. See you!

Lesson 25 What's the Weather Like Today（Ⅰ）

(In class)

Jack: How is today, Anna?

Anna: I feel fine today.

Jack: I already know that you've recovered and are in good health.

Anna: Then what were you asking about?

Jack: I was asking about the weather.

Anna: Mmm..., it looks fine to me.

Jack: What is the highest air temperature?

Anna: I don't know.

Jack: Didn't you listen to the weather forecast?

Anna: How could I understand?

Jack: Let's go and ask our professor then.

Anna: Professor Wang, how can we understand the weather forecast?

Professor Wang: Oh, that's easy. I happen to have the recording of today's weather forecast with me here. You can listen to it.

Anna: That's terrific.

Hello, dear listeners. We are now broadcasting the weather forecast for the cities in the next 24 hours. For Beijing, it will be turning from cloudy to overcast tonight. There will be drizzling. The lowest temperature will be 20 degrees centigrade. During the daytime tomorrow, it will be turning from cloudy to clear. The wind speed will be 2 to 3 on the Beaufort scale. The highest temperature will be 28 degrees centigrade.

Professor Wang: Do you understand?
Jack: Just a little.
Anna: I don't understand a bit of it.
Professor Wang: Don't worry. If you listen to it a few more times, you will surely be able to understand it.

Lesson 26 What's the Weather Like Today (II)

(After class)
Jenny: Jack, look, it looks as if it's going to rain.
Jack: Didn't you say that the weather forecast said that it would not rain today?
Yamaguchi: Jenny said that it would be fine today.
Jenny: The weather forecast said exactly that. How come that the weather has changed without any warning?
Jack: Our teacher said that Beijing's weather is noted for being scorching and rainy in summer, cold and dry in winter and arid and windy in spring.
Yamaguchi: Autumn is the best season in Beijing, with no wind and little rain, being neither cold nor hot.
Jenny: I forgot what our teacher said. It is the rainy season now and we have to take our raincoats with us when going out.
Yamaguchi: And we are riding our bicycles. How can we go back to the university then?
Jack: I know what to do. Please follow me.

Jack: Miss, we are caught in the rain and we have not taken our rain gear with us. Can you lend it to us?
Shop assistant: Of course. What would you like, a raincoat or an umbrella?
Jack: We are riding our bicycles, so we prefer raincoats.
Shop assistant: That's fine.
Jack: When do we have to return them?
Shop assistant: You can bring them back when you come to the store next time.

Jack: Do we have to return them to this store?

Shop assistant: Oh, no. There are dozens of shops in this city that offer this service. You can send them to a shop that's the nearest to your place.

Jack: Thank you!

Jenny: Jack, you seem to know that young lady very well.

Jack: No, I don't know her at all.

Jenny: Then how do you know that she would lend rain gear to you?

Jack: My Chinese friends told me that I could borrow rain gear from stores.

Yamaguchi: Aren't they afraid that the borrowers would not return them?

Jack: "Civilized Umbrellas" are for public use, and they trust that everybody carries out civilized conducts.

Lesson 27 Going Sightseeing in Beijing（I）

(In class)

Professor Wang: Hello, everybody. How long have you been in Beijing?

Jack: It has been almost a year since I came to Beijing.

Jenny: For me, it's less than half a year.

Professor Wang: Have you gone sightseeing in Beijing yet?

Jack: Jenny and I did it quite often.

Professor Wang: What about Yamaguchi?

Yamaguchi: I have roamed around Beijing for several times by taxi.

Jack: You call that roaming around? You should go sightseeing by bike.

Yamaguchi: I don't know the way. I am afraid I can't find my way home if I go by bike.

Jenny: Why not ask someone to lead the way?

Yamaguchi: Who should I ask then?

Jack: Me. I am already a veteran Beijinger.

Professor Wang: Jack, you said that you were already a veteran Beijinger?

Jack: Well, that's embarrassing. I was just cracking a joke.

Professor Wang: Do you know Beijing well?

Jack: I can't say I do, but I won't get lost if I go by bike.

Yamaguchi: What's your trick then?

Jack: That's simple. Beijing's streets, lanes and roads are all straight, either going north and south, or east and west.

Jenny: As long as one remembers the location of our university, one won't lose the way.

Yamaguchi: That won't do. I can't orient myself.

Jack: There is another way. Just remember turning left, and then right...

Yamaguchi: No, no, one turn after another will surely get me confused.

Jenny: Yamaguchi, then you'd better spend money to take a taxi. You will not get confused in a taxi. Ha, ha, ha...

Lesson 28 Going Sightseeing in Beijing (II)

(After class)

Yamaguchi: Jack, where are we off to?

Jack: First to Wangfujing, then to Dashilanr at Qianmen and Xidan.

Yamaguchi: Why shall we go to these places?

Jenny: Because they are the three most bustling business streets in Beijing.

Yamaguchi: Good, let's go. I'll follow you two.

Jack: In front of us is Wangfujing. Let's park our bikes here, and it will be easy for us to collect them when we leave.

Yamaguchi: Oh, it's really a bustling scene. There are so many shops here, one after another.

Jenny: Listen, what is the man over there crying out? "Please stop to have a look. Buy one and get one free!" "Markdown sale for a new season!"

Jack: I don't quite understand him. It sounds like he's urging you to stop and buy his stuff.

Yamaguchi: Let's go and have a look.

Jack: Here is North Xidan Street.

Yamaguchi: It is different from Dashilanr, but similar to Wangfujing.

Jenny: Dashilanr is a traditional business street, narrow with antique shop fronts.

Jack: Both Xidan and Wangfujing are modern business streets with magnificent tall buildings.What a dignified air!

Jenny: In these stores, you can buy almost anything that's available anywhere in the world.

Yamaguchi: Really? Is all the merchandise imported?

Jack: No, imported or domestic, everything is being sold here, and everything is being bought here.

Jenny: China is really populous, with lots of shops and lots of goods. Whatever is offered for sale is being bought. It's easy to do business and make money here.

Yamaguchi: Judging by the way you spoke, you seemed to have earned a lot of money on the Chinese market.

Jack: Ha, congratulations and may you make a fortune!

Jenny: The same to you!

生词总表

Vocabulary List

生词	拼音	课号
A		
啊	à	2
哎呀	āiyā	21
挨	āi	28
爱	ài	11
爱人	àiren	3
安娜	Ānnà	1
安排	ānpái	9
安全	ānquán	17
安全带	ānquándài	8
B		
八（8）	bā	5
芭比娃娃	Bābǐ wáwa	17
把	bǎ	20
吧	ba	8
白天	báitiān	25
百（100）	bǎi (yìbǎi)	7
拜访	bàifǎng	23
办	bàn	18
办法	bànfǎ	26
办公室	bàngōngshì	5
半	bàn	9
帮助	bāngzhù	13
保证	bǎozhèng	21
杯	bēi	12
北	běi	27
北海公园	Běihǎi Gōngyuán	27
北京大学	Běijīng Dàxué	13
北京饭店	Běijīng Fàndiàn	6
本市	běn shì	26
笔直	bǐzhí	27
必须	bìxū	26
变	biàn	18
变	biàn	26
遍	biàn	25
标准间	biāozhǔnjiān	6
别	bié	6
别人	biérén	13
冰箱	bīngxiāng	24
病	bìng	19
播送	bōsòng	25
不过	búguò	12
不	bù	2
不管	bùguǎn	17
C		
才	cái	13
操场	cāochǎng	18
层	céng	23
茶	chá	12
差	chà	9

差不多	chàbuduō	28
长城饭店	Chángchéng Fàndiàn	13
常	cháng	22
潮湿	cháoshī	26
吵（架）	chǎo (jià)	26
称	chēng	15
称呼	chēnghu	4
城市	chéngshì	25
橙汁（儿）	chéngzhī (r)	12
吃	chī	16
迟到	chídào	19
抽烟	chōu yān	15
出差	chūchāi	20
出口	chūkǒu	28
出来	chūlái	21
出门	chūmén	26
出租车	chūzūchē	8
传统	chuántǒng	28
窗户	chuānghu	17
春天	chūntiān	26
次	cì	13
从	cóng	17
存	cún	28
错	cuò	5

D

打	dǎ	5
打的	dǎdī	8
打工	dǎgōng	21
打针	dǎzhēn	20
大	dà	10
大家	dàjiā	11
大街	dàjiē	27
大名	dàmíng	4
大娘	dàniáng	13
大厦	dàshà	28
大栅栏	Dàshílànr	28
大夫	dàifu	20
带	dài	21
带路	dàilù	27
单人间	dānrénjiān	6
耽误	dānwu	22
但是	dànshì	13
蛋糕	dàngāo	10
当	dāng	11
当然	dāngrán	12
倒是	dàoshì	28
到	dào	8
到底	dàodǐ	27
的	de	3
得	de	12
得体	détǐ	14
得	děi	12
等	děng	6
低	dī	19
低头	dītóu	17
地方	dìfang	27
地址	dìzhǐ	23
第	dì	22
点	diǎn	7
点	diǎn	9
电	diàn	17

电话	diànhuà	5
电脑	diànnǎo	17
电视	diànshì	24
掉	diào	15
丢	diū	27
东	dōng	27
东西	dōngxi	14
冬天	dōngtiān	26
懂	dǒng	25
都	dōu	11
堵车	dǔchē	8
肚子	dùzi	19
短信	duǎnxìn	5
对	duì	2
对不起	duìbuqǐ	2
兑换	duìhuàn	7
多	duō	17
多少	duōshao	7
多云	duōyún	25

E

俄罗斯	Éluósī	2
二（2）	èr	5

F

发	fā	5
发财	fācái	28
发票	fāpiào	8
发烧	fāshāo	19
发现	fāxiàn	17
发炎	fāyán	20
法国	Fǎguó	2
法语	Fǎyǔ	11
繁华	fánhuá	28
方便	fāngbiàn	18
方向	fāngxiàng	27
芳名	fāngmíng	4
房间	fángjiān	6
房租	fángzū	23
飞机	fēijī	20
分	fēn	7
分	fēn	9
分	fēn	27
风	fēng	25
风力	fēnglì	25
夫人	fūrén	2
服务台	fúwùtái	6
服务员	fúwùyuán	11
付	fù	23
附近	fùjìn	23

G

该	gāi	14
该死	gāisǐ	22
改天	gǎitiān	24
干旱	gānhàn	26
干吗	gànmá	24
干燥	gānzào	26
感冒	gǎnmào	19
刚	gāng	8
刚才	gāngcái	7
港币	gǎngbì	7
高	gāo	25
高兴	gāoxìng	2

高亚安	Gāo Yà'ān	4
告诉	gàosu	13
个	gè	6
各地	gè dì	28
给	gěi	5
跟	gēn	26
更	gèng	19
工作	gōngzuò	12
公交车	gōngjiāochē	17
公里	gōnglǐ	8
公司	gōngsī	5
公寓	gōngyù	23
恭候	gōnghòu	6
恭喜	gōngxǐ	28
购物	gòuwù	14
古色古香	gǔsè-gǔxiāng	28
顾客	gùkè	14
挂	guà	10
拐	guǎi	27
怪	guài	21
怪不得	guàibude	24
管理	guǎnlǐ	12
光	guāng	20
光临	guānglín	6
广告	guǎnggào	16
逛	guàng	27
贵	guì	16
贵姓	guìxìng	4
国	guó	2
国产	guóchǎn	28
过	guò	9
过	guo	16

H

哈	hā	12
嗨	hēi	1
害	hài	22
寒冷	hánlěng	26
韩国	Hánguó	2
汉堡	hànbǎo	18
汉语	Hànyǔ	11
好	hǎo	1
好像	hǎoxiàng	10
号码	hàomǎ	5
喝	hē	12
嗬	hē	28
和	hé	11
黑板	hēibǎn	16
很	hěn	1
后	hòu	5
后天	hòutiān	6
胡同	hútòng	27
糊涂	hútu	27
互相	hùxiāng	11
华氏温度	Huáshì wēndù	19
化妆品	huàzhuāngpǐn	28
话	huà	11
坏	huài	19
欢迎	huānyíng	12
还	hái	10
还	huán	26
还是	háishi	7
环境	huánjìng	23
换	huàn	7
换季	huànjì	28

回	huí	10
回来	huílái	5
汇率	huìlǜ	7
会	huì	12
火车	huǒchē	20
货	huò	15

J

几乎	jīhū	18
机票	jīpiào	18
级	jí	25
记得	jìde	12
系	jì	8
季节	jìjié	26
家	jiā	10
家庭影院	jiātíng yǐngyuàn	24
家用电器	jiāyòng diànqì	24
价（格）	jià (gé)	15
检查	jiǎnchá	20
简单	jiǎndān	15
见面	jiànmiàn	21
讲	jiǎng	26
讲究	jiǎngjiu	20
交	jiāo	11
角（毛）	jiǎo (máo)	7
叫	jiào	4
叫外卖	jiào wàimài	18
教室	jiàoshì	5
接	jiē	22
接待	jiēdài	24
接通	jiētōng	17
街（道）	jiē (dào)	28
节	jié	21
节省	jiéshěng	20
杰克	Jiékè	1
介绍	jièshào	3
借	jiè	26
今天	jīntiān	6
斤	jīn	15
金钱	jīnqián	20
近	jìn	23
进	jìn	4
进口	jìnkǒu	28
经费	jīngfèi	20
经济	jīngjì	12
经理	jīnglǐ	2
九（9）	jiǔ	5
久	jiǔ	27
久仰	jiǔyǎng	4
酒	jiǔ	12
酒吧	jiǔbā	12
就	jiù	9
橘子	júzi	15
句	jù	13
觉得	juéde	21

K

咖啡	kāfēi	12
开车	kāichē	8
开除	kāichú	22
开始	kāishǐ	13
砍	kǎn	15
看	kàn	14

看样子	kàn yàngzi	25
考（试）	kǎo (shì)	13
咳嗽	késou	19
可口可乐	Kěkǒu Kělè	12
可能	kěnéng	19
可是	kěshì	11
可以	kěyǐ	6
渴	kě	19
刻	kè	9
客气	kèqi	6
课本	kèběn	21
肯	kěn	26
恐怕	kǒngpà	24
口	kǒu	19
口气	kǒuqì	28
口语	kǒuyǔ	21
口子	kǒuzi	16
苦	kǔ	20
快	kuài	10
矿泉水	kuàngquánshuǐ	12

L

拉	lā	19
拉开	lākāi	17
来	lái	6
懒	lǎn	18
劳驾	láojià	13
老百姓	lǎobǎixìng	24
老板	lǎobǎn	12
老大爷	lǎodàye	13
老家	lǎojiā	18
老头儿	lǎotóur	13
了	le	6
冷	lěng	26
离开	líkāi	17
里（边）	lǐ (bian)	23
礼貌	lǐmào	13
礼物	lǐwù	18
厉害	lìhai	20
俩	liǎ	21
练习	liànxí	14
凉快	liángkuai	26
量	liáng	19
两	liǎng	15
辆	liàng	9
聊	liáo	17
了解	liǎojiě	11
咧	lie	16
零（0）	líng	5
零下	língxià	25
刘亮	Liú Liàng	12
留学生	liúxuéshēng	3
留言	liúyán	5
六（6）	liù	5
楼	lóu	22
录音	lùyīn	25
路	lù	13
旅行	lǚxíng	7
啰	luo	16

M

麻烦	máfan	22
马路	mǎlù	18
马上	mǎshàng	24

吗	ma	1
嘛	ma	20
买	mǎi	10
卖	mài	15
慢	màn	20
没关系	méi guānxi	2
没有	méiyǒu	8
美国	Měiguó	2
美元	měiyuán	7
门口	ménkǒu	9
门脸儿	ménliǎnr	28
门面	ménmiàn	28
们	men	3
蒙人	mēng rén	15
秘书	mìshū	2
免	miǎn	4
免费	miǎnfèi	24
名片	míngpiàn	23
名字	míngzi	4
明白	míngbai	11
明天	míngtiān	6

N

拿	ná	21
哪	nǎ	2
哪	na	10
哪里	nǎli	25
哪儿	nǎr	8
内销	nèixiāo	28
那	nà	3
那（么）	nà (me)	11
男	nán	3
南	nán	27
难	nán	14
呢	ne	1
能	néng	14
嗯	ǹg	14
你	nǐ	1
年	nián	10
您	nín	4
努力	nǔlì	12
女	nǚ	3
暖和	nuǎnhuo	26

O

哦	ò	7
欧元	ōuyuán	7

P

怕	pà	20
旁边	pángbiān	18
跑	pǎo	12
陪	péi	19
赔钱	péiqián	22
朋友	péngyou	3
啤酒	píjiǔ	12
便宜	piányi	16
片	piàn	20
漂亮	piàoliang	10
品牌	pǐnpái	24
平房	píngfáng	24
苹果	píngguǒ	15
瓶	píng	12
葡萄	pútao	15

葡萄酒	pútaojiǔ	12
普及	pǔjí	17
普通	pǔtōng	24

Q

七（7）	qī	5
欺骗	qīpiàn	16
其实	qíshí	18
奇怪	qíguài	21
骑	qí	26
起床	qǐchuáng	22
起价	qǐjià	8
气派	qìpài	28
气温	qìwēn	25
千（1000）	qiān (yìqiān)	7
前门	Qiánmén	28
前天	qiántiān	6
钱	qián	7
钱富成	Qián Fùchéng	20
巧	qiǎo	24
亲爱的	qīn'ài de	10
亲眼	qīnyǎn	24
清（楚）	qīng (chu)	27
晴	qíng	25
请	qǐng	4
请假	qǐngjià	19
请求	qǐngqiú	13
秋天	qiūtiān	26
取	qǔ	28
取消	qǔxiāo	10
去	qù	8
缺点	quēdiǎn	16

R

然后	ránhòu	28
让	ràng	13
热	rè	26
热闹	rènao	28
人	rén	2
人民币	rénmínbì	7
认识	rènshi	2
日	rì	10
日本	Rìběn	2
日语	Rìyǔ	11
日元	rìyuán	7
日子	rìzi	10
容易	róngyì	14
如果	rúguǒ	21

S

三（3）	sān	5
嗓子	sǎngzi	19
山口	Shānkǒu	3
商场	shāngchǎng	26
商店	shāngdiàn	18
商业	shāngyè	28
上班	shàngbān	9
上车	shàng chē	8
上课	shàngkè	17
上面	shàngmiàn	23
上网	shàngwǎng	18
上星期	shàng xīngqī	10
稍	shāo	6
（摄氏）度	(shèshì) dù	19

身体	shēntǐ	25
生活	shēnghuó	18
生气	shēngqì	10
生日	shēngrì	10
生意	shēngyi	8
声	shēng	13
师傅	shīfu	9
十（10）	shí	5
什么	shénme	4
时候	shíhou	6
时间	shíjiān	20
实体	shítǐ	24
食堂	shítáng	18
史特凡	Shǐtèfán	22
使用	shǐyòng	17
世界	shìjiè	28
市场	shìchǎng	28
事	shì	5
试	shì	13
是	shì	2
收费	shōu fèi	24
手	shǒu	15
手表	shǒubiǎo	21
手机	shǒujī	5
售货员	shòuhuòyuán	14
书	shū	3
舒服	shūfu	19
熟	shóu	26
熟悉	shúxi	27
甩卖	shuǎimài	28
双人间	shuāngrénjiān	6
双休日	shuāngxiūrì	20
谁	shéi/shuí	2
水	shuǐ	19
睡觉	shuìjiào	20
睡懒觉	shuì lǎnjiào	18
顺便	shùnbiàn	26
顺利	shùnlì	22
说	shuō	3
说明	shuōmíng	17
司机	sījī	8
四（4）	sì	5
四合院	sìhéyuàn	24
送	sòng	10
宿舍	sùshè	5
算	suàn	7
随便	suíbiàn	12
随时	suíshí	18
岁	suì	15
所以	suǒyǐ	21

T

他	tā	2
它	tā	21
她	tā	2
太	tài	11
太太	tàitai	3
套	tào	23
套间	tàojiān	6
特点	tèdiǎn	26
特快列车	tèkuài lièchē	22
特色	tèsè	24
疼	téng	19
提醒	tíxǐng	18

体温	tǐwēn	19
体温表	tǐwēnbiǎo	20
体验	tǐyàn	24
替	tì	10
天	tiān	10
天安门	Tiān' ān Mén	27
天气	tiānqì	25
甜	tián	16
挑（选）	tiāo (xuǎn)	16
条	tiáo	28
跳	tiào	17
听	tīng	12
听力	tīnglì	21
听众	tīngzhòng	25
停车	tíngchē	8
同事	tóngshì	3
同屋	tóngwū	23
同学	tóngxué	3
同志	tóngzhì	13
突然	tūrán	17
退	tuì	20

W

外	wài	23
外（边）	wài (bian)	23
完成	wánchéng	18
玩儿	wánr	11
玩笑	wánxiào	27
晚	wǎn	21
晚点	wǎndiǎn	22
万（10000）	wàn (yíwàn)	7
万文杰	Wàn Wénjié	4
王	Wáng	6
网	wǎng	24
往	wǎng	27
忘	wàng	10
危险	wēixiǎn	17
微信	wēixìn	18
为	wèi	14
为了	wèile	11
为什么	wèi shénme	10
位	wèi	26
喂	wèi	5
文化	wénhuà	24
文明	wénmíng	26
问	wèn	4
问题	wèntí	7
我	wǒ	1
五（5）	wǔ	5
误会	wùhuì	14

X

西	xī	27
西单	Xīdān	27
西瓜	xīguā	15
习俗	xísú	24
洗衣机	xǐyījī	24
喜欢	xǐhuan	11
下班	xiàbān	9
下车	xià chē	8
下课	xiàkè	19
下星期	xià xīngqī	10
夏天	xiàtiān	26
先	xiān	11

鲜花	xiānhuā	10
现代化	xiàndàihuà	18
现金	xiànjīn	7
现在	xiànzài	9
(相)信	(xiāng) xìn	16
香蕉	xiāngjiāo	15
享受	xiǎngshòu	18
想	xiǎng	11
向	xiàng	27
项	xiàng	26
小贩	xiǎofàn	15
小姐	xiǎojiě	1
小时	xiǎoshí	9
效劳	xiàoláo	14
些	xiē	24
写	xiě	16
谢文	Xiè Wén	2
谢谢	xièxie	1
新闻	xīnwén	18
信息	xìnxī	24
星期	xīngqī	10
星期二	xīngqī èr	10
星期六	xīngqī liù	10
星期日(星期天)	xīngqīrì (xīngqītiān)	10
星期三	xīngqī sān	10
星期四	xīngqī sì	10
星期五	xīngqī wǔ	10
星期一	xīngqī yī	10
行	xíng	9
幸会	xìnghuì	4
姓	xìng	4
休息	xiūxi	20
学生	xuésheng	2
学习	xuéxí	11
雪	xuě	25

Y

亚运村	Yàyùncūn	23
炎热	yánrè	26
羊肉串	yángròuchuàn	21
吆喝	yāohe	28
药	yào	20
要	yào	6
要紧	yàojǐn	20
要是	yàoshi	14
也	yě	1
一(1)	yī	5
医院	yīyuàn	19
一定	yídìng	13
一共	yígòng	16
一路	yílù	20
一切	yíqiè	22
一下	yíxià	3
颐和园	Yíhé Yuán	27
已经	yǐjīng	9
以后	yǐhòu	9
以前	yǐqián	11
以为	yǐwéi	21
一点儿	yìdiǎnr	13
一起	yìqǐ	14
意思	yìsi	11
阴	yīn	25
银行	yínháng	7

饮料	yǐnliào	12
应该	yīnggāi	13
英镑	yīngbàng	7
英国	Yīngguó	2
英语	Yīngyǔ	11
用	yòng	9
优点	yōudiǎn	16
邮局	yóujú	8
友谊商店	Yǒuyì Shāngdiàn	8
有	yǒu	5
有空儿	yǒu kòngr	23
有事儿	yǒu shìr	14
有效	yǒuxiào	17
又	yòu	14
右	yòu	23
娱乐	yúlè	23
雨	yǔ	25
雨具	yǔjù	26
雨伞	yǔsǎn	26
雨衣	yǔyī	26
预报	yùbào	25
预订	yùdìng	6
遇到	yùdào	22
遇上	yùshàng	24
元（块）	yuán (kuài)	7
原来	yuánlái	21
约会	yuēhuì	10
月	yuè	10
越来越	yuè lái yuè	18

Z

再	zài	13
再见	zàijiàn	5
在	zài	5
糟糕	zāogāo	21
早	zǎo	21
早上	zǎoshang	1
怎么	zěnme	4
怎么样	zěnmeyàng	15
窄	zhǎi	28
占线	zhànxiàn	5
站	zhàn	17
站	zhàn	21
着急	zháojí	25
找	zhǎo	8
这	zhè	2
这么	zhème	22
这儿	zhèr	12
这样	zhèyàng	13
着	zhe	16
真	zhēn	12
整	zhěng	9
正点	zhèngdiǎn	22
正好	zhènghǎo	25
正宗	zhèngzōng	16
挣钱	zhèng qián	21
支票	zhīpiào	7
知道	zhīdào	5
职员	zhíyuán	22
只	zhǐ	13
志愿者	zhìyuànzhě	24
智能	zhìnéng	18
中国	Zhōngguó	2
钟	zhōng	9

周末	zhōumò	10
朱丽亚·利维	Zhūlìyà Lìwéi	2
住院	zhùyuàn	20
注意	zhùyì	18
转	zhuǎn	5
赚钱	zhuàn qián	21
准备	zhǔnbèi	9
自己	zìjǐ	11
自行车	zìxíngchē	26
字	zì	16
总	zǒng	9
总裁	zǒngcái	12
总是	zǒngshì	22
走	zǒu	12
昨天	zuótiān	6
左	zuǒ	23
作业	zuòyè	18
坐	zuò	4
做	zuò	8

nghua

ua	uo	uai	ui	uan	un	uang	ueng	ü	üe	üan	ün
wa	wo	wai	wei	wan	wen	wang	weng	yu	yue	yuan	yun
	duo		dui	duan	dun						
	tuo		tui	tuan	tun						
	nuo			nuan				nü	nüe		
	luo			luan	lun			lü	lüe		
	zuo		zui	zuan	zun						
	cuo		cui	cuan	cun						
	suo		sui	suan	sun						
zhua	zhuo	zhuai	zhui	zhuan	zhun	zhuang					
chua	chuo	chuai	chui	chuan	chun	chuang					
shua	shuo	shuai	shui	shuan	shun	shuang					
rua	ruo		rui	ruan	run						
								ju	jue	juan	jun
								qu	que	quan	qun
								xu	xue	xuan	xun
gua	guo	guai	gui	guan	gun	guang					
kua	kuo	kuai	kui	kuan	kun	kuang					
hua	huo	huai	hui	huan	hun	huang					

普通话声韵拼合总表

Combinations of Initials and Finals in Puto[illegible]